ADVANCE

for

Finding the Jewel in Job Loss

Rich Jensen isn't writing in theory; he's been there. *Finding the Jewel in Job Loss* is an intensely personal and practical book that comes from Rich's own experiences. I especially appreciate that it is rich in Scripture. When Rich Jensen lost his ministry, he turned to God's Word and drew from its deep wells of truth, encouragement and help. I heartily recommend this book for anyone who is dealing with difficulties in tough economic times.

Pastor Ronald L. Kohl
Senior Pastor, Grace Bible Fellowship Church
Quakertown, PA

I cannot endorse this work strongly enough. In these challenging economic times in which few of us have not been impacted, either directly or indirectly, there exists a dearth of works that encourage us from a biblical perspective. Discouraging commentaries abound, whether in print or in cable and national news reports, related to the diminishing employment rates. Most reading this have either personally experienced the pain and humiliation of job loss or have close friends and/or family members that have. It is easy to become disheartened when one's livelihood is stripped away suddenly and unexpectedly.

However, and in spite of the bleakness of the situation, now a work that sparkles as a jewel reflecting beautiful sunlight has been provided. In his *Finding the Jewel in Job Loss*, Richard Jensen offers words of hope, encouragement and even inspiration. Writing from personal experience and as a dedicated Christian striving to see the hand of God in such tragic circumstances, Jensen walks the reader through biblical passages and concepts that major on many of the basics of the faith. These basics are what keep each of us focused on the heart and plan of God even in the midst of life's difficulties. He ultimately shows that unemployment should bring the Christian back to full faith and trust in God. And what may surprise many readers are his revelations of how unemployment can even be used as a ministry tool for the greater glory of God.

Kudos Richard! We need this encouraging light in these dark economic days.

Tony Guthrie, Ph.D.
Assistant Professor of Preaching
Pastoral Ministry Director of Doctoral Studies
Luther Rice Seminary

Rich Jensen has done all of us in the marketplace a tremendous favor! He has wonderfully exposed the issue that all of us must work through, whether facing job loss or not. God is trying to drive home the heart issues of identity and priority in our career experience. Thank you, Rich, for getting right to the heart of the matter! This is a great book that all should read.

Lee Truax, President
Christian Business Men's Connection (CBMC) Inc.
Chattanooga, TN

For believers who find themselves in the difficult position of being out of work, Rich Jensen has written an encouraging and thoroughly biblical guidebook. It does more than help them find their next job, it helps them find their lives.

As a pastor who has walked the road of losing a job, he offers a way to see God at work for good in the loss. If you or someone you know has or is walking this frustrating, hopeless and painful road, Jensen's book will help navigate the path in a God honoring way.

Rev. Richard C. Langton
Executive Director
Workplace Chaplains US

Finding the *JEWEL* in Job Loss

Walking by Faith in Unemployment

Richard S. Jensen

CLC PUBLICATIONS

Fort Washington, PA 19034

Finding the Jewel in Job Loss:
Walking by Faith in Unemployment

Published by CLC Publications

U.S.A.
P.O. Box 1449, Fort Washington, PA 19034

GREAT BRITAIN
51 The Dean, Alresford, Hants SO24 9BJ

AUSTRALIA
P.O. Box 469, Kippa-Ring QLD 4021

NEW ZEALAND
118 King Street, Palmerston North 4410

Printed in the United States of America

First printing April, 2011

ISBN-10: 1-936143-15-1
ISBN-13: 978-1-936143-15-3

To Cindi
who has remained strong and steadfast;

To my children, Natalee and Stephen,
who are learning the character and names of God
by experiencing firsthand
through the journey of everyday life
His faithfulness, provision, sufficiency and so much more;

To the God and Father of our Lord Jesus Christ,
who has proven He is the God of all comfort;

and

To my God and Savior, Jesus Christ,
who has promised that His grace is sufficient
and His power is made perfect in weakness.

May this book give glory to God
as I boast all the more gladly of my weaknesses.

Contents

Foreword

I've never hunted for gems, but I've heard you can do that in Tennessee. I've seen billboards along Interstate 75 luring would-be prospectors to grab a shovel and strike it rich. And from what I've heard, any gemstones you dig up, you can claim. Of course, you have to purchase a ticket to get into the quarry, but once you're inside, the loot you find is yours to keep.

Not many people would ever think that losing your job would be a quarry ticket—a place where precious gems could be unearthed. That sounds more like a billboard promise than a biblical reality. However, in this rare treatment Richard will do more than make vague promises to prospecting disciples. He will prove that there are jewels to be discovered in what most would consider an unpromising and unproductive place in life.

Take your time. This book is more than a slap on the back and a hurried "Don't worry, everything will work out as soon as you start digging." Instead, Richard will carefully expound on Scripture as he leads you through the maze of unemployment and uncertainty as well as empathize through insights from his own experience.

Most importantly, Richard will help you handle with honesty both the obstacles and opportunities for those who seek the lasting treasures of Christ's glory. And you'll be prepared to turn around and help newcomers who've just shown up with their own shovels . . . they'll need to learn where to hunt for treasure too.

Stephen Davey
Pastor/Teacher, Colonial Baptist Church
President, Shepherds Theological Seminary

Introduction

Beginning the Journey

It was a typical Monday morning, with nothing to indicate that I was about to begin a journey—one that would teach me valuable lessons on walking by faith.

I was working in my office, responding to some e-mails and looking over my agenda for the day, when there was a knock on my door. I looked up and saw the senior pastor standing in the doorway. He asked if we could talk for a moment.

As I listened to him speak, my mind began to swirl. Did he really just say what I thought he said? No, there must be a mistake. This couldn't possibly be happening. When he finished what he had to say and left, I just continued to sit there. Every muscle in my body seemed heavy and sluggish. I continued to say over and over, "How can this be?" I still remember that day like it was yesterday; the vivid scene is etched in my memory.

I had just been informed that my position was going to be eliminated. It wasn't based on my job performance; I was simply the victim of a financial downturn. The budget numbers did not line up with the giving numbers. Unless the Lord God chose to miraculously provide, there would need to be significant cuts, including my position.

As I continued to sit there in my office on that Monday morning, my thoughts changed to "How will I break this news to my family? How will I tell my children?" And the most looming question on my mind: "What do I do now?"

"This is just a bad nightmare; I am going to wake up any moment now!" I said to myself. "How could this be happening to me?" I had started the journey through unemployment.

The day finally came when, on a Sunday afternoon, I stood in my office for the last time. There had been many tears—not only from my wife and me, but from many of the church members as well. I gathered the last of the boxes of my personal belongings and, before shutting off the light, turned around for one final look. It all seemed surreal. "This is just a bad nightmare; I am going to wake up any moment now!" I said to myself. "How could this be happening to me?" I had started the journey through unemployment.

The world economy is in the midst of a major economic downturn. According to government estimates, the current (January 2011) unemployment rate in the United States hovers around ten percent, the highest in almost thirty years. This represents nearly sixteen million individuals out of work. The number of the long-term unemployed (those out of work for six months or more) is escalating at alarming rates.

Long-term unemployment is particularly draining, both emotionally and spiritually. It is a journey filled with potholes and hazardous turns, and requires patience and trust in God. For most people entering unemployment, the main goal is survival—getting by until you find a new job and get back on the road to success. But I want you to consider taking a different approach.

We use the phrase "diamond in the rough" to refer to someone with hidden potential, just as the true beauty of a natural diamond is hidden until it is cut and polished. This book does not downplay the pain of job loss. Unemployment can bring the strongest of us to our knees, and nothing in this or any other book can eliminate the emotional struggle of being downsized. But *Finding the Jewel in Job Loss* reveals some of the treasures which await the child of God who walks by faith, trusting and depending upon Christ Jesus the Lord. It seeks to show how the difficult trials in life are God's way of completing the cutting and polishing process so that we will shine more brilliantly as lights in the world (Phil. 2:15).

The challenge before us is to see unemployment as a season in life where God is at work "to will and to work for his good pleasure" (Phil. 2:13).

Like diamonds in the rough, the beauty of trials like job loss is also hidden; we can see it only by embracing the reality that the greatest lessons in life are those with eternal significance. I have experienced the stress of an unknown future and the burden of figuring out where the money will come from to pay the bills. Yet the challenge before us is to see unemployment as a season in life where God is at work "to will and to work for his good pleasure" (Phil. 2:13). His will is that we be conformed more to the likeness of His Son, Jesus Christ. It is then that we shine as lights, displaying the brilliant jewel of true salvation before others.

Embracing this truth means dismissing the notion that our best life is now. God's revealed will has nothing to do with obtaining a better job or even becoming a better person. God's Word makes it abundantly clear that His will for our lives is growth in holiness and righteousness (1 Thess. 4:3; Eph. 4:24). This book has no magic formula for eliminating trials and makes no false assurance that you will get a job if you just have more faith. This book is intended to guide you to something of far greater worth.

If you have received Jesus Christ the Lord, you have the most precious jewel already—Christ in you, the hope of glory (Col. 1:27). The trials of life are the cutting and polishing process which God uses to mold and shape us so that the glory of His Son shines more clearly from our lives. This is the jewel in job loss.

If you have lost your job and are in the midst of the job search, take heart! You are a diamond in the rough—and God is at work.

Section One

The Jewel of True Identity

During my journey of unemployment, some close friends treated our family to a day at a local amusement park. Our son, we discovered, has a real love for roller coasters, and he asked me to join him.

The first part of the ride wasn't bad. After leaving the station, we began the long climb to the top. I knew what was coming next and was bracing myself for it, but before I was totally ready, the train of cars hurtled down the tracks at seventy miles an hour, only to jerk back up, then down again, to the left and then the right. We descended in a corkscrew and went over a couple of smaller hills before sailing back into the station. The ride lasted about two minutes.

After we got off the ride (and my knuckles regained some color), I began to think about what I had just experienced. A roller coaster is the perfect metaphor for the experience of job loss. The only problem is that this particular roller coaster lasts a lot longer than two minutes!

Part of the ride is coming to understand what really defines us as persons. Unemployment has a way of tearing down the very things we use to shape our identity. From the rubble that remains, we can then address the issues of what truly molds us into who we are. This is the first facet of the jewel we can discover in job loss.

I was not expecting the emotional turmoil that arrived with my first day of unemployment. As the rays of dawn began streaming through the windows, I was already dressed and ready for a new day. Then the thought hit me: What do I do? Where do I go?

Fear and anxiety began to grip my heart. The weight of figuring out how I would provide for my family increased exponentially, until my knees felt weak and my heart began to pound. Where and when would all this end?

My thoughts shifted from my unknown future to my immediate past. What would I have been doing if I still had my job? A deep gloom began to overshadow my heart. There were no meetings to attend, no projects to be completed, no events to prepare. There was nothing. For so long my identity had been associated with what I did, but now that was gone.

Looking at the pieces of my shattered image, I began to wonder, "How do I put the pieces back together? What will the new picture look like?"

Finally I asked the question at the root of it all: "Who am I?"

Chapter One

Exposing the Identity Shapers

For ten years I only knew one job. It didn't even cross my mind to consider doing something else. After the initial shock and disillusionment of my termination, I diligently started the job search process. I did all the things you are instructed to do, such as updating my résumé and honing my interviewing skills. I lined up the key documents and began to fill out the endless stream of applications.

At first there is a lot of energy and excitement as you consider the possibilities—a new job with new challenges, maybe even a new career direction. Things change, though, when doors of opportunity begin to close: excitement gives way to self-doubt and questioning of your purpose in life. This is the beginning of the identity crisis. The longer you are on this journey, the more critical it is to understand who you truly are—a process which requires some real soul-searching.

Let's begin the process by looking at four major ways in which people seem to define themselves. A person's identity is usually shaped by at least one, and often more than one, of these beliefs.

Identity Shaper 1: You Are What You Do

This belief is the number one identity-shaper among men. One of the first questions a man asks another man he meets for the first time is "What do you do for a living?" For many men losing a job means losing a core way in which they see themselves.

One of the first questions a man asks another man he meets for the first time is "What do you do for a living?" For many men, losing a job means losing a core way in which they see themselves.

Why do we tend to link our identity with what we do? One reason might be the sheer number of hours invested in a career or occupation: the typical job involves forty to fifty hours per week. For many workers, it is not uncommon to spend sixty or more hours a week at their job—about forty percent of one's life. How can anything that consumes so much time not have a profound impact on a person's identity?

Identity Shaper 2: You Are Who You Know (and Who Knows You)

A second major source of identity formation is social relationships—deriving one's sense of self from group affiliation and interaction. As long as a group is not harmful or abusive, there is nothing sinful about identifying with a certain social network. In fact, the Scriptures present the church as a social network—as a family, a body, a covenant people—and emphasize the good which comes from being united to this community. What happens, however, if rejection or separation occurs from the social network in which you found your greatest identity?

Peer pressure is not just an adolescent problem, and it can be a powerful influence on how we view ourselves. Many people speak of building a reputation or leaving a legacy, which is simply another way of saying that they want to be known and accepted by their social network. To be known and accepted is part of the very fabric of our humanity. Therefore, it is natural for us to have our identity shaped by who we know and are known by. If the relationship crumbles, the results can be devastating.

Identity Shaper 3: You Are What You Know

We live in an information age. The perception today is the more information you have, the better off you are. Only a few generations ago a high school education was the minimum needed to get a good paying job. My generation was told to get a college degree to be assured of a living wage. Things continue to trend upward. In many professions you now need a master's degree to earn a decent salary. On-the-job training and continuing education are also demanded by many occupations.

Related to this is the specialization of knowledge. Consider the field of medicine. When I was a kid, our family doctor was a general practitioner. Look at the health care landscape today: there are few, if any, physicians practicing "general" medicine. I am grateful for advancements in health care, but it illustrates the point that education has become increasingly specialized. As a result, one's education can become a significant source of one's identity.

Identity Shaper 4: You Are What You Have

Many derive their identity from their possessions or financial portfolio. In this materialistic culture the driving influence in marketing is the insatiable appetite to get the latest, the best, the biggest. This is the "keeping up with the Jones'" mentality.

For example, owning a house can be a very wise investment—until discontentment sets in. A young family may start out in a small townhouse or condo, but the cultural pressure to tie their sense of self-worth to the things they possess may lead them to purchase a home two or three times larger. This can continue to spiral out of control, until it is not the size of the house but finding identity in the house which is the issue. When you are willing to strap yourself and your family with a mortgage you cannot financially handle, you have moved beyond the basic necessity of providing shelter.

This applies as well to home furnishings and decorations, cars, computers, media devices and gadgets—they all become "must have" items. A friend of mine once pointed out that the wants of the previous generation become the "needs" of the next generation. A simple illustration of this point is air conditioning. It's a wonderful invention, and I enjoy the comfort it brings as much as anyone else. But aside from those with certain types of health issues, is air conditioning a necessity? If so, how did previous generations (or the vast majority of earth's population today, for that matter) survive without it? It is so easy to rely on a new gadget to the point that we convince ourselves it is a need and not merely a convenience. The more this lifestyle is fed, the more our possessions shape how we see ourselves.

Unemployment: The Identity-Buster

The road of unemployment can devastate one's sense of identity; downsizing can really bring one down to size. The challenge is that every one of our worldly identity shapers may be shaken or even stripped away by the loss of one's job. I wasn't prepared for the identity-busting effect of unemployment, and the further I traveled down this path, the more I saw how deeply entrenched was my dependence on these worldly attitudes for my identity.

When the very sources which shaped your identity begin to crumble, it will lead you to despair and depression, or to a foundation which is rock-solid and can weather any storm.

For most men the dominant identity shaper seems to be occupation, and once it is taken away, the other aspects of identity formation are also threatened. Losing one's job can threaten the identity-shaper of possessions because now you don't have the same income to maintain what you have. It can threaten the identity-shaper of knowledge because often your job is based on what you know. It can threaten the identity-shaper of social networks because your job is often the key to entering certain networks, the source of much of your social contact and the foundation on which a legacy or reputation is built. When unemployment strikes, your whole identity can be shattered.

All across our land is the carnage of the devastating effects of basing one's identity on these very fragile components. When the very sources which shaped your identity begin to crumble, it will lead you in one of two places: to despair and depression, or to a decision to base your identity on a foundation which is rock-solid and can weather any storm. One treasure of unemployment is coming to the point where we see that there is more to life than our job, possessions, academic degrees or social network.

The struggle to find one's identity is a universal problem. Since our hearts are inclined to find identity in such things as occupation, wisdom, possessions and social connections, the first step to victorious living is to realize just how meaningless and empty these identity shapers are. There is one book of the Bible which speaks specifically and extensively on this issue.

The Meaninglessness of Identity Shapers

The book is Ecclesiastes and the author, simply known as "the Preacher, the son of David, king of Jerusalem" (Eccles. 1:1), is someone who "had it all" yet came to realize how futile it is to build one's identity on any of it.

Throughout the book the Preacher repeatedly uses a word which means vanity, meaninglessness or emptiness. This word exposes the futility and uselessness of the object. In other parts of the Old Testament, it refers to idols, but in Ecclesiastes this single word is used over thirty-five times to give shape to the book's central theme: that all the things in which the world seeks to find meaning, significance and purpose are in the end meaningless.

Ecclesiastes peers through all these things and exposes their shallowness. In a very methodical way, the Preacher tears down each of the identity shapers.

What You Do

He proclaims that if you shape your identity upon what you do, it is pointless, because there is a day coming when it will be taken away: "I hated all my toil in which I toil under the sun, seeing that I must leave it to the man who will come after me, and who knows whether he will be wise or a fool? Yet he will be master of all for which I toiled and used my wisdom under the sun. This also is vanity" (2:18–19).

If your job or career is not taken away through downsizing or dismissal, it will eventually be taken away by means of retirement or death. All the effort and pride you put into that occupation will be handed over to another who may or may not have the same work ethic or goals you possessed. Like it or not, the day is coming when someone else will be the "master of all you worked for."

The Preacher also emphasizes how the stress and sleepless nights related to work are meaningless: "What has a man from all the toil and striving of heart with which he toils beneath the sun? For all his days are full of sorrow, and his work is a vexation. Even in the night his heart does not rest. This also is vanity" (2:22–23).

Worry does not produce anything worthwhile. It only produces sorrow with a side order of ulcers and high blood pressure. The pacing back and forth, anxiety and stress only creates emotional and spiritual chafing which leaves you raw, sore and irritated. Isn't this what we do though? Work is the primary cause of the greatest amounts of heartache and sorrow, yet it is also the one thing which we seek to define who we are. Where is the meaning in this?

Does this mean we are not to care about our work or the quality in which we do it? Absolutely not! We are to labor and toil for the glory of God (1 Cor. 10:31). Whatever occupation or job you have, you are to do it to the best of your ability and in the name of the Lord Jesus (Col. 3:17). Ecclesiastes is drawing our attention to how meaningless and empty it is to find identity in what we do. Our identity must be grounded upon something of much greater worth and stability than a career.

Who Knows You

Closely linked with "what you do" is the legacy you leave. Not only will your occupation be handed down but your accomplishments and successes will also be handed over to someone who did not put the sweat and tears into them that you did. You put all the work into building it up, yet someone else is going to build on top of it: "Sometimes a person who has toiled with wisdom and knowledge and skill must leave everything to be enjoyed by someone who did not toil for it. This also is vanity and a great evil" (2:21).

We think of ourselves as indispensable to the company we work for. This is where a reality check is very much needed.

What makes this statement even more stinging is that we often think more highly of ourselves than we ought to. We think that without us everything will fall apart. We think of ourselves as indispensable to the company we work for. This is where a reality check is very much needed. For most of us, we were hired to take a position that someone else did before us and someone else will do after us. Life goes on.

This might seem harsh; and it is. But that is the point. This is why it is meaningless and foolish to link one's life occupation with one's identity.

What You Know

It is also deceptive to derive identity from one's knowledge or wisdom. The Preacher concludes that in the end there is little difference between the fool and the one with wisdom.

> I saw that there is more gain in wisdom than in folly, as there is more gain in light than in darkness. The wise person has his eyes in his head, but the fool walks in darkness. And yet I perceived that the same event happens to all of them. Then I said in my heart, "What happens to the fool will happen to me also. Why then have I been so very wise? And I said in my heart that this also is vanity. For of the wise as of the fool there is no enduring remembrance, seeing that in the days to come all will have been long forgotten. How the wise dies just like the fool! (2:12–16).

The Preacher does not say it is foolish to pursue wisdom. Ecclesiastes is part of the wisdom literature of the Old Testament, and wisdom is a major concern of this book. Wisdom is the essence of living right or living well. It is the culmination of daily decisions based upon the precepts and principles derived from God's Word. Therefore, wisdom should be the pursuit of all God's people. The Preacher himself will come back to looking at the benefit of wisdom over folly again and again in Ecclesiastes (7:1–29; 9:11–10:20).

What is foolish is making the pursuit of wisdom a primary identity-shaper. This is the irony of the issue. While wisdom is worthwhile for living well, it becomes worthless when pursued for defining identity. How can that be? When the dust settles, what happens at the end for the fool is the same for the wise. In other words, both the wise and the fool die in the end. If one's whole identity is wrapped around the knowledge and wisdom gained in this life, what long-term gain is there? "For what does it profit a man to gain the whole world [including all wisdom and knowledge] and forfeit his soul?" (Mark 8:36).

What You Have

It is vanity to find personal identity and significance in our occupation, our reputation, our wisdom or our knowledge. It is also futile to form our identity around wealth and possessions. The Preacher had tremendous wealth. He would have topped the chart of the Forbes 400 list of wealthiest people. He owned sprawling estates containing the most beautiful gardens and plantations. Consider his assessment of materialism:

> I made great works. I built houses and planted vineyards for myself. I made myself gardens and parks, and planted in them all kinds of fruit trees. I made myself pools from which to water the forest of growing trees. . . . I also gathered for myself silver and gold and the treasure of kings and provinces. . . . And whatever my eyes desired I did not keep from them. . . . Then I considered all that my hands had done and the toil I had expended in doing it, and behold, all was vanity and striving after wind, and there was nothing to be gained under the sun (2:4–6, 8, 10–11).

Wealth is a driving passion within our culture. We glamorize the rich and famous. If we are honest, there are many times we dream what it would be like to have the wealth of men like Bill Gates or Warren Buffett. There is a great temptation to idolize those who have achieved high levels of prosperity, but "he who loves money will not be satisfied with money, nor he who loves wealth with his income; this also is vanity" (5:10).

The pursuit of wealth and financial success actually eats away at the person and can even become emotionally and physically detrimental (5:13–14). The most grievous injustice is that in the end you can't take any of it with you. The Preacher put it this way: "As he came from his mother's womb he shall go again, naked as he came, and shall take nothing for his toil that he may carry away in his hand. This also is a grievous evil: just as he came, so shall he go, and what gain is there to him who toils for the wind?" (5:15–16).

Not only are you not able to take the riches with you upon death, but the pursuit of financial wealth can actually be the cause of your death. "Moreover, all his days he eats in darkness in much vexation and sickness and anger" (5:17). The more you have, the more you will tend to worry and stress over how you will maintain it. There is no rest. There is only the penchant thirst for more.

Just as with work, reputation and wisdom, there is nothing inherently evil about wealth. Money itself is neutral. What is sinful is the attitude one has toward money. If the passion of your life is to climb the ladder of financial success for the purpose of obtaining whatever material possessions you want, this is an indication you are a lover of money. If you cling tightly to your possessions and are unwilling to make sacrifices in income or possessions, you have an unhealthy attachment. It is the love of money that is the root of all kinds of evil (1 Tim. 6:10).

The inclination of the human heart is discontent. There is a restlessness in always seeing the grass as being greener on the other side.

Challenging the deeply ingrained mindset of equating success with wealth is a difficult topic to address. It flies in the face of the American dream. It is counter-cultural. We live in one of the wealthiest countries in the world. Even those citizens who live below the poverty line in this country are in a far better economic condition than most of the rest of the world. Yet the inclination of the human heart is discontent. There is a restlessness in always seeing the grass as being greener on the other side. Our hearts are not easily satisfied. We continually strive to advance to the next level. This insatiable appetite to rise in economic status is what creates vexation in the heart. Even if you get to the heights of economic prosperity, there is the fear of losing it.

Would it not be more beneficial for the advancement of the Kingdom if the followers of Christ develop what John Piper calls a "war-time lifestyle"?

There is a war going on in the world between Christ and Satan, truth and falsehood, belief and unbelief. It tells me there are weapons to be funded and used, but that these weapons are not swords or guns or bombs but the gospel and prayer and self-sacrificing love (2 Cor. 10:3–5). And it tells me that the stakes of this conflict are higher than any other war in history; they are eternal and infinite: heaven and hell, eternal joy or eternal torment (Matt. 25:46).

I need to hear this message again and again, because I drift into a peacetime mind-set as certainly as rain falls down and flames go up. I am wired by nature to love the same toys that the world loves. I start to fit in. I start to love what others love. I start to call earth "home." Before you know it, I am calling luxuries "needs" and using my money just the way unbelievers do. I begin to forget the war.[1]

We must untangle ourselves from the idea that success is linked with prosperity. The first step in this process is to see the meaninglessness of pursuing the world's riches, wealth and possessions.

Through the journey of unemployment, the Lord Jesus taught me to detach myself from finding identity in things such as occupation, possessions and knowledge. God opened my eyes to see the meaningless of these things. We must tear down these facades. We must inevitably link our identity with something, so this begs the question: what is it that gives significance to our life? What truly reveals our ultimate identity? In the end, after all has been heard, "Fear God and keep his commandments, for this is the whole duty of man" (Eccles. 12:13–14). When we come to see this, we are in a prime position to walk in closer intimacy with Jesus.

Chapter Two

Discovering One's True Identity

One evening during family devotions my daughter wanted to pray specifically for a couple of job interviews I had scheduled. Little did I realize the emotional reaction this simple, thoughtful gesture would trigger in me. As we bowed our heads, a numbness came over me. Whenever I attempted to pray out loud, I choked up and began to cry. I had reached a breaking point. I was emotionally and spiritually exhausted.

Long-term unemployment (job loss lasting twenty-six weeks or longer) can put you on the verge of hopelessness and despair. To live victoriously in a God-honoring way, we need to cling to the truth and promises revealed to us in God's Word. While Peter's advice to "Preach the word . . . reprove, rebuke, and exhort" (2 Pet. 4:2) refers primarily to public preaching, sometimes we also need to preach the gospel to ourselves. Whatever the season of life, but especially when we are afflicted, we must recall and meditate upon the glory of God in the face of Christ Jesus. This is not easy; it will take discipline.

Why is this necessary, especially when traveling the road of unemployment? The gospel reminds us of our new identity in Christ. When plagued with stress and trouble, we often discover that our biggest enemy is us. We repeatedly fall back into the subtle trap of linking our identity with the identity shapers so prized by the world. To combat this we must continually remind ourselves of our true identity—an identity not based on externals, not governed by circumstances, but determined by what God thinks of us.

From God's perspective there are only two groups of people in the world. The Word of God uses contrasting terms like the unsaved and the saved (Eph. 2:8; John 3:17), the lost and the found (Luke 15:24; 19:10), those in darkness and those in the light (John 8:12; 12:46). To be transformed from the old identity of being unsaved, lost children of darkness into the new identity of being the saved, found children of light is solely by the sovereign grace of God. This is a precious and blessed treasure. When we repent and believe in Christ alone, our identity is transformed, by God's grace, into a new creation in Christ.

Identity Crisis

The end of the last chapter left us with an unresolved problem. While the duty of man is to fear God and keep His commandments (Eccles. 12:13), this is not what we naturally choose to do. We choose to do what is right in our own eyes, in rebellion against God's commandments.

This flies in the face of how we naturally see ourselves; we don't want to think we are lost or bad. The human heart is naturally inclined to view itself as good, and our culture reinforces this. From every angle we are taught that man is inherently good—or at the very least, morally neutral—and that what we call good and evil are merely learned responses to his environment. This is another identity shaper prevalent in our culture.

From a spiritual perspective it is the actions, motives and inclinations of the heart which expose our true identity.

The Word of God, however, gives the consistent testimony that the nature of man is inherently corrupted by sin. Man is not good; man is depraved. Scripture uses many different terms to define man's natural identity, such as the flesh (Rom. 8:5–8), the natural man (1 Cor. 1:14), unrighteousness (1 Pet. 3:18), spiritual blindness (Isa. 42:16) and spiritual death (Eph. 2:1; Col. 2:13).

From a spiritual perspective it is the actions, motives and inclinations of the heart which expose our true identity. We all are born with a sin nature. This is the wellspring of walking in the ways of the world and of rebellion against God's law (Heb. 3:7–11; Col. 1:21; Eph. 2:2). Not only are we guilty of not keeping God's commandments, we also have no natural inclination to do so. Consider Romans 3:10–20:

> None is righteous, no, not one; no one understands; no one seeks for God. All have turned aside; together they have become worthless; no one does good, not even one. . . . There is no fear of God before their eyes.
>
> Now we know that whatever the law says it speaks to those who are under the law, so that every mouth may be stopped, and the whole world may be held accountable to God. For by works of the law no human being will

be justified in his sight, since through the law comes the knowledge of sin.

As the Preacher says, "surely there is not a righteous man on earth who does good and never sins (Eccles. 7:20). Therefore, based on our works we stand condemned. Without saving grace, this is our identity before God.

Even our knowledge of spiritual things is also darkened. We are not able to understand or see the light of the gospel of the glory of Christ (2 Cor. 4:4). Man is without knowledge of the true and living God (John 1:10; 1 John 3:1). The reason man's knowledge is futile and empty stems from his rejection of God the Creator. Man chooses not to honor God or give Him the thanks due His name (Rom. 1:18–23). This impacts the way in which we live:

> Now this I say and testify in the Lord, that you must no longer walk as the Gentiles do, in the futility of their minds. They are darkened in their understanding, alienated from the life of God because of the ignorance that is in them, due to their hardness of heart. They have become callous and have given themselves up to sensuality, greedy to practice every kind of impurity. (Eph. 4:17–19)

In comparison, to live the new life in Christ is evidenced in righteousness, holiness and God-honoring ways (Eph. 4:22–24). The apostle Paul repeatedly links one's knowledge of spiritual things with one's true identity. Apart from being united to Jesus Christ, man's identity is marked by alienation from God and, therefore, from God's perspective we are born "sons of disobedience."

What a blow to our self-esteem! But unless we accept the truth of our identity as fallen humans, we will never understand why a new identity in Christ is such good news. Which brings us to a crucial question: how can our fallen identity be changed?

There is only one way to receive this new identity. Jesus Himself said, "I am the way, and the truth, and the life. No one comes to the Father except through me" (John 14:6). One's identity is transformed from death to life at the moment he or she receives Christ as Lord.

> For God so loved the world, that he gave his only Son, that whoever believes in him should not perish but have eternal life. For God did not send his Son into the world to condemn the world, but in order that the world might be saved through him. Whoever believes in him is not condemned, but whoever does not believe is condemned already, because he has not believed in the name of the only Son of God. (John 3:16–18)

This is the message of the gospel, the good news we must preach to ourselves daily.

Weathering the storms of life and growing in our faith requires turning from the very things which gave us a false assurance of our identity.

A trial like unemployment strips away the façade of seeing ourselves through the lenses of the culturally informed identity shapers of what we do, what we know, who we know and what we have. Trials and hardships strip away any pretense of thinking more highly of ourselves than we ought. It is in the midst of the confusion and upheaval of life, when things seem to be their darkest, that we are able to see most clearly the light of the glory of God in the face of Jesus Christ (2 Corinthians 4:6).

Weathering the storms of life and growing in our faith requires turning from the very things which gave us a false assurance of our identity. It is critical to remember we possess a corrupt and depraved nature, but it is also important to know our new identity in Christ, as those who have turned from sin to serve the living and true God by faith.

The Christian's New Identity

First Peter was written to those who were trusting in Christ alone, but were experiencing hardship and suffering. To encourage those whose faith may have begun to waver, Peter begins by stressing their new identity, which is only found by being "in Christ" (2 Cor. 5:17). In the same way, we can live victoriously in the midst of joblessness if we focus on a biblical identity. The first five verses of First Peter provide a good foundation for understanding the basis of a new Christ-centered identity.

I Am an Elect Exile!

Peter addresses the letter "to those who are the elect exiles" (1:1) He wastes no time in informing them who they are in Christ. To be named among "the elect" refers to the fact that we were chosen by God: "He chose us in him before the foundation of the world, that we should be holy and blameless before him. In love he predestined us for adoption as sons through Jesus Christ, according to the purpose of his will" (Eph. 1:4–5).

Election is solely by the mercy and grace of God (Rom. 9:10–16). It is not based upon man's works or knowledge.

Remember, we are all born as children of wrath (Eph. 2:3). There is nothing in our natural-born identity which would make us want to know God. Therefore salvation is by the sovereign choice of God and is the free gift of God (Eph. 2:8–9).

The heart of man desires to boast in his accomplishments, works or knowledge, and within man is the insatiable desire to be self-sufficient and self-reliant. But the essence of grace is unmerited kindness and favor from God. Grace obliterates the identity-shaping shrines which we tend to erect. I can't boast in my goodness. I can't boast in my knowledge. I can only boast in Christ.

We are also exiles—strangers, sojourners, pilgrims. What is the significance of this aspect of our new identity in Christ? It provides a proper perspective on how we ought to regard this world and the things in it. We are now free from the burdening ways in which the world labels and defines us. Our heavenly Father and our King have changed our status forever. As elect exiles, we now have citizenship in heaven (Phil. 3:20); this world is not our home, and we journey through this life toward our eternal home where

> . . . no longer will there be anything accursed, but the throne of God and of the Lamb will be in it, and his servants will worship him. They will see his face, and his name will be on their foreheads. And night will be no more. They will need no light or lamp or sun, for the Lord God will be their light, and they will reign forever. (Rev. 22:3–5)

Unemployment is only one small step in the overall journey toward our eternal home. If we have believed in the

Lord Jesus Christ, we may have lost our job, but we have not lost our identity. No matter what is stripped away, I boast in nothing but Christ and Him crucified (1 Cor. 2:2). To live a God-honoring life in the midst of unemployment, or any other trial, is to joyfully proclaim, "for to me to live is Christ, and to die is gain" (Phil. 1:21). This is the motto of the elect exiles.

Walking with Jesus by faith makes possible the ability to live well in the pain and burdens presented in the job search. So as you travel along the road of unemployment—filling out applications, sending résumés and following up from interviews—know that your ultimate identity is not linked with getting the job you desire. You might even need to take a job which is not what you consider ideal. Remember: this is only part of the journey. To persevere requires keeping your eyes focused on your true identity and your eternal destiny: You are an elect exile!

I Am Heir and Co-Heir with Christ!

Another aspect of our identity in Christ is our inheritance in Him:

> Blessed be the God and Father of our Lord Jesus Christ! According to his great mercy, he has caused us to be born again to a living hope through the resurrection of Jesus Christ from the dead, to an inheritance that is imperishable, undefiled, and unfading, kept in heaven for you, who by God's power are being guarded through faith for a salvation ready to be revealed in the last time. (1 Pet. 1:3–5)

We are given the rights and privileges to the Father's inheritance. The legal claim of an heir was of paramount importance in times of antiquity. It also can have tremendous impact today as well.

Knowing we are fellow heirs with Christ gives us hope and strength to persevere through the trials along the journey.

What if an attorney called to say that you were named as sole heir to a multi-billionaire's estate? How would this news change your long-term plans? How would it alter your financial decisions? And yet, such a windfall is paltry at best compared to the inheritance we have in Christ Jesus. It would not equal even a single grain of sand on the endless shoreline of spiritual blessings which are kept in heaven for us in Christ Jesus (Eph. 1:3). Knowing we are fellow heirs with Christ gives us hope and strength to persevere through the trials along the journey.

In just five verses Peter bolsters our confidence to handle the rejection letters, the employment applications that never receive a response, and the endless days of job hunting with no apparent progress. There will still be tough days and painful setbacks, but if our focus is on eternity, based on our identity in Christ, we can continue to live with hope, even without work. In addition to being elect exiles and co-heirs with Christ, First Peter also calls us a chosen race, a royal priesthood, a holy nation and a people for God's own possession (2:9). Knowing our eternal identity is in Christ leads to great rejoicing, even if you have to suffer awhile through trials such as unemployment (1:6–9).

Such a focus is not a denial of the real pain and hardship caused by unemployment and other trials. This is not an exercise in empty platitudes or the "power of positive think-ing." It is instead the only hope that can penetrate deep into our soul to heal the wounds in a way that empty words and clichés never can. It provides the power to lift our drooping hands and strengthen our weakened knees. The answer is to look to Jesus, the author and perfecter of our faith, and the foundation of our identity as a new creation (Heb. 12:1–12; Gal. 6:15). There is no simple formula for learning this key to a victorious and God-honoring life. It requires a daily clinging to the promises of the gospel and the riches of our new identity in Christ.

Jesus Christ: The Identity Changer

The gospel is a message of transformation—the good news of a changed identity. "If anyone is in Christ, he is a new creation" (2 Cor. 5:17). Those with this new identity are united with Christ Himself. They are elect exiles, children of God, co-heirs with Christ. But all these rich treasures of a new identity in Christ, along with every other "spiritual blessing in the heavenly places" (Eph. 1:3), are only for those who have heard and believed the gospel message.

The gospel can be summarized in two core statements. First, "Christ died for our sins in accordance with the Scriptures" (1 Cor. 15:3). Left to ourselves we remain dead in our sins and are deserving of condemnation and judgment (John 3:18). But Jesus Christ, the eternal Son of God, became a man and laid down His life, being crucified on a cross to cancel the record of debt we owed to God for our sin and rebellion (Col. 2:13–14).

The second core statement of the gospel is that Christ Jesus "was buried, that he was raised on the third day" (1

Cor. 15:4). This is the foundation of our hope. It is through Christ's resurrection that the victory over sin and death was secured. If Christ had not risen from the dead, our faith and identity as Christians would be meaningless (1 Cor. 15:12–28).

So what must one do to be saved? Conversion is a total change in one's identity and involves two essential actions: repentance and faith. Repentance means a change of mind, a turning around. Repentance is turning from the ways of sin, from what seems right in your own eyes, and turning to God, and what pleases Him.

The second aspect of conversion is faith—believing in your heart that God raised Jesus from the dead. Saving faith involves trust—relying alone on the finished work of Christ for redemption and reconciliation with God the Father. The glorious good news of Jesus Christ is that upon repentance and faith our identity is changed; we are new creations in Christ.

This means Jesus Christ is far more than just another identity-shaper; He is the identity-changer. Unlike the identity-shapers of the world, our new identity in Christ is not based on "what we do" but upon what Christ has already accomplished; our identity is "created after the likeness of God in true righteousness and holiness" (Eph. 4:24). It is not based on "what we know"; our new identity in Christ is "the new self, which is being renewed in knowledge after the image of its creator" (Col. 3:10).

Our new identity in Christ is also not based on "what we have." The treasures of this world have no eternal value. Only one treasure is of lasting worth: Christ Jesus the Lord. When we come to see Christ as our greatest treasure, then we can say, "whatever gain I had, I [count] as loss for the sake of Christ. Indeed, I count everything as loss because of the surpassing worth of knowing Christ Jesus my Lord" (Phil. 4:7–9). After all, "where your treasure is, there your heart will be also" (Matt. 6:21).

The jewel in all of life, the pearl of great value, is "Christ in you, the hope of glory."

Our identity is based, however, on "who knows us"—we are known by God the Father. In His amazing grace He drew us to Himself; by the washing of regeneration and renewal of His Holy Spirit we are born again (John 12:32; Titus 3:5). We are now fellow heirs with Christ (Rom. 8:17; Titus 3:7), the adopted children of God (John 1:12–13; Gal. 4:5) and servants of the Most High God (Eph. 6:6; Rev. 22:3). We once were not a people, but now we are the people of God (1 Pet. 2:9; Rev. 21:3).

This new identity in Christ changes everything, and nothing can take it away. The jewel in all of life, the pearl of great value, is "Christ in you, the hope of glory" (Col. 1:27; Matt. 13:44–46).

If I take my eyes off Jesus, the anchor of my soul, I am tossed back and forth by the waves of circumstance; when I rest in the knowledge of who I am in Him, I have peace and contentment. Living without work is a difficult journey, filled with many pitfalls. It is amazing how easily we can fall back into defining ourselves by such things as occupation, possessions and knowledge, which only leads to discouragement and depression. But with Christ as our anchor, we can weather any storm.

Just as the brilliance of a diamond is more visible against a dark background, the jewel of Christ in us is more visible to the world when put against the darkness of life's trials. So then, during this season of unemployment, we need to let the light of the gospel penetrate and saturate every aspect of our lives, "for God, who said, 'Let light shine out of darkness,' has shone in our hearts to give the light of the knowledge of the glory of God in the face of Jesus Christ" (2 Cor. 4:6). Our lives are like empty jars of clay. When we come to saving faith, we are filled with the treasure of Christ, "to show that the surpassing power belongs to God and not to us" (2 Cor. 4:7).

Take time to meditate on what the Bible says about your new identity in Christ. As you spend time in God's Word, take note of all the ways the people of God are described, and be strong and courageous. As you walk by faith through unemployment, keep your eyes on our Lord and Savior, and "Do not turn from [God's Word] to the right hand or the left, that you may have good success wherever you go" (Josh. 1:6–7).

Section Two

The Jewel of Sanctification

How we handle unemployment is one way we can shine our light before others and grow in likeness to Christ. The process of becoming more like Christ—sanctification— is rarely pleasant, yet it is precious and valuable.

This section looks at four aspects of our character which the Lord develops as we walk by faith: humility, content- ment, joy and perseverance. When these are present in our lives, against the backdrop and darkness of hardship, we will shine as lights in the world (Phil. 2:15).

These and other character traits of the Christ-centered life are interrelated. To learn one lesson is the springboard to learning the others. At the core of these four characteristics is a right perspective of our identity in Christ. If our identity is skewed by the world's values, it will affect our perception of all these characteristics. But when our identity is rooted in our union and fellowship with Jesus, beholding the glory of the Lord, we are transformed more and more into His likeness (2 Cor. 3:18).

This transforming process will take deadly aim at all the

posturing of our prideful hearts, exposing our self-centeredness and self-sufficiency. It will lead us to renewed repentance, in which we confess our pride and in humility depend
upon the grace of God in all circumstances. The sanctification process will also expose the depth of our discontentment. But if we rest in our identity in Christ and find our
delight in Him, it will fill us with an inexpressible joy which
overflows in an attitude of thankfulness, praise and gladness.
We will then find the strength to persevere through the trial
of unemployment.

Chapter Three

Growing in Humility

What causes a stock market crash? One cause is known as a market correction. A period of rapid economic growth can cause stock prices to soar far above th eir real market value. Such inflated prices are bound to come down eventually—and when they do, it isn't a pretty sight.

A similar process needs to happen in our spiritual lives as well. There are times when our lives are rolling along nicely, and the skies couldn't look brighter. Things are going so well for us that an inflated sense of self-sufficiency and self-worth emerges. We begin to think more highly of ourselves than we ought (Rom. 12:3).

Then something such as unemployment hits and takes the wind out of our sails, leaving us drifting in a sea of confusion. It can even lead to bitterness and resentment. But the maturing believer learns to see trials as spiritual "market corrections." They are the trigger points to reform the perspective we have of ourselves.

John Stott wrote that "at every stage of our Christian

development and in every sphere of our Christian discipleship, pride is our greatest enemy and humility is our greatest friend."[1] Pride is relying on self, while humility is trusting and depending upon God. When pride begins to dominate, a spiritual correction is needed. This is one important lesson in the God-honoring life.

From the moment of our birth, there is a continual dripping of pride—leaving the deposits of self-sufficiency, self-worth and self-gratification. Over time this creates a calloused and petrified heart.

The road of unemployment is filled with twists and turns, and no one knows what lies beyond the next curve. Along this path I often found myself trusting in my own strength, abilities and knowledge. After all, we can't sit back and do nothing; there are job applications to fill out, résumés to send, job fairs to attend and interviews to go to. It is not "spiritual" to expect God to drop a job into our lap. On the other hand, true godliness is also not summarized by "God helps those who help themselves"—a proverb by Ben Franklin which, incidentally, has no support whatsoever in Scripture. Humility is doing what you can but depending on God to sustain and provide. Humility is surrendering every aspect of the job search to Christ.

I approach this chapter with great trepidation because I know I still have much to learn in the area of humility. I have often slipped and lost my footing on this point. Unemployment is a continual reminder to all of us of our absolute need to depend upon the sovereignty and goodness of God. The longer the Lord keeps us waiting, the more He exposes the pride in our hearts.

A couple of years ago my family visited a limestone cave to see the formation of stalagmites and stalactites. The constant dripping of mineral and calcium deposits over hundreds of years creates these huge underground configurations. A similar process takes place in the recesses of our hearts. From the moment of our birth, there is the continual dripping of pride—leaving the deposits of self-sufficiency, self-worth and self-glorification. Over time this creates a calloused and petrified heart.

The prophet Ezekiel referred to this as a "heart of stone": "And I will give them one heart, and a new spirit I will put within them. I will remove the heart of stone from their flesh and give them a heart of flesh, that they may walk in my statutes and keep my rules and obey them. And they shall be my people, and I will be their God" (Ezek. 11:19). The first step in this process is to see our own heart of stone—the pride that resides in each of us.

Unveiling a Heart of Pride

Both a warning and a promise are contained in the verse "God opposes the proud but gives grace to the humble" (1 Pet. 5:5). The warning is serious: God opposes the proud. It isn't that God is merely disappointed or displeased with them—He is intent on bringing them down. It is just as important, however, to know the promise that God gives grace to the humble.

What does it mean to be proud? What does it mean to be humble? We need to know the answer to these questions if we want to heed the warning and claim the promise. We need to understand the nature of pride and humility if we want to receive the spiritual correction to be found in trials such as unemployment.

A good definition of both pride and humility is found in Psalm 20:7: "Some trust in chariots and some in horses, but we trust in the name of the Lord our God." In the psalmist's day chariots and horses symbolized the height of military strength. The most basic definition of pride is boasting in one's self-sufficiency or self-reliance. The deeply rooted pride of the human heart rears its ugly head in boasting of one's accomplishments, position, ability, resources, intellect and even righteousness.

Pride is trusting in the "chariots and horses" of identity shapers. Placing our confidence and reliance in strength, ability and resources reveals a self-sufficient and self-promoting heart. This attitude is a subtle trap of *trusting* in self instead of *denying* self (Luke 9:23).

Pride takes away from giving God the glory. It neglects or openly refuses to recognize that our complete dependence is upon the Lord. Pride gives praise and honor to the wrong object, glorifying the gift and not the Giver of all good gifts (James 1:17).

Pride also deceives. For example, what makes an above average musician? Is it just natural ability and diligent practice? What about success in the business world? Is it just fortitude, hard work and intuition? What is missing is the awareness and acknowledgement of God's universal blessings. Pride deceives us into thinking it is our doing and not the work of the One who created us.

Matthew 5:45 states that God the Father "makes his sun rise on the evil and on the good, and sends rain on the just and on the unjust." This is known as common grace—the principle that God pours out blessing upon all people, regardless of who they may be: "Everyone to whom God has given wealth and possession and power to enjoy them, and to accept his lot and rejoice in this toil—this is the gift of God" (Eccles. 5:19). To take credit for what God has given us is sin. Boasting exalts our ability or gifts without recognizing our dependence on God. It is taking the credit for our successes, when God deserves the praise. Boasting always leads to self-glorification and self-exaltation.

Pride distorts reality. God sovereignly gives and takes away as He wills (Job 1:21). "The earth is the Lord's and the fullness thereof, the world and those who dwell therein" (Ps. 24:1). Therefore, there is nothing in which man has a right to boast. Yet our world is filled with the proud and the arrogant, who boast in what they have done, what they have, what they know and who they know. They refuse to give praise and glory to the Lord who gave it (Rom. 1:18–23). They continue to exalt and glorify their own name. In fact, are we not all guilty of this?

Pride also leads to a misplaced focus. It focuses on the self, and makes a person think more highly of himself and of his own interests and agenda (Rom. 12:3; Phil. 2:3–4). Pride makes one think his ways are always best, his needs the most important, his problems the most serious. It leads to each of us doing what is right in our own eyes (Judg. 21:25).

It is easy to become inwardly focused in the midst of difficult trials and ignore the hardships of others around us. One day while I was wallowing in self-pity over the struggle to find a job, I received an e-mail about a member of our previous church who was having serious health issues. This was the wake-up call I needed. God opened my eyes to see that I had become consumed with thinking only of myself and my problems. This is as much pride as touting one's own successes.

Pride is a universal problem which blinds and deceives everyone. It springs forth in different forms and at varying times. It can rear its head when one is at the top as well as when one is at the bottom.

Pride is a universal problem which blinds and deceives everyone. It springs forth in different forms and at varying times. It can rear its head when one is at the top as well as when one is at the bottom. Pride is at the center of the sin nature which we all possess and which we continue to battle with in the depths of our hearts.

A Picture of True Humility

I have found it necessary to discuss pride in such detail because it is so deeply rooted in our hearts. The "heart is deceitful above all things, and desperately sick" (Jer. 17:9), and we are quick to rationalize our sin. Pride is the basic condition of fallen humanity. "The sad fact is that none of us are immune to the logic-defying, blinding effects of pride," notes C.J. Mahaney. "Though it shows up in different forms and in different degrees, it infects us all. The real issue is not if pride exists in your heart; it's where pride exists and how pride is being expressed in your life."[2]

To get the complete picture, however, it is just as important to discuss humility—a God-glorifying, Christ-exalting,

Spirit-dependent, eternally focused and outwardly interest-ed perspective. As pride exalts self, humility exalts Christ. As pride glories in its own accomplishments, humility glorifies God. As pride focuses on self-interest, humility focuses on the interests of others. Jesus Christ is the perfect example of true humility.

If pride is an obsession with oneself, then the key to vic-tory over it is to "look not only to [one's] own interests, but also to the interests of others" (Phil. 2:4). We must have the "same mind" as Christ. In other words, we must develop the same "attitude" and "way of thinking" which was character-istic of Jesus. Just as this is true for harmony and unity to ex-ist in the church, this is also necessary for the God-honoring life in the midst of trials. To shine as lights in the darkness of unemployment requires surrendering our rights and privi-leges, and considering the needs of others.

Surrendering Our Rights and Privileges

Consider the irony of our condition. We have no privi-leges or rights we can demand of God. He is the Creator; we are His creation. He is the great, majestic and sovereign Lord of the universe; we were formed from the dust of the earth. The only reason for our existence is the grace of God. To our shame we exalt ourselves and demand rights and privileges which we do not own.

In contrast Jesus is of the same essence, eternally equal with the Father in power and glory. Yet to His glory and praise, even after weighing the facts, He did not cling to His glory, but allowed it to be veiled when He took on flesh.

Christ modeled perfect humility in not thinking highly of Himself. He had every right as the Son of God to do so, but chose not to demand His divine rights or the privileges of Deity. Take time and let this sink in: Jesus, "though in the form of God, did not count equality with God a thing to be grasped" (Phil. 2:6). "Form" refers to the essence of Christ. The very essence and substance of Jesus is Deity. The fullness of God was pleased to dwell in Christ Jesus (Col. 1:19), yet He did not consider His divine glory as a treasure to cling onto at all costs.

Jesus is the Word and had every right to retain the external glory of His majesty which He had throughout all eternity. Yet in His humiliation Jesus willingly and voluntarily took on flesh and chose to dwell among men (John 1:14) and subject Himself to the same pains, hardships and temptations common to man. This is humility: surrendering your rights and privileges, giving them up to the glory of God.

It is possible to develop an entitlement mentality in the workplace, thinking you deserve a certain type of job or a certain salary. As week after week goes by with no job, you may begin to feel irritated, even violated, and find yourself stammering "It's not fair." But who says we "deserve" a particular position? How did we get to the point where we expect God to give us the ideal job? What if, in His infinite wisdom, God decides it is better for us not to have what we think we deserve? Perhaps God wants to use this season in life to train us in surrendering our rights and privileges. To come to this point is to learn to live well.

Considering the Needs of Others

Humility is a calling to surrender not only our rights, but also our self-focus. Jesus came not to be served, but to serve (Matt. 20:28; Mark 10:45). The majestic and glorious

Son of God "made himself nothing, taking the form of a servant" (Phil. 2:7).

Why would Jesus willingly veil the fullness of His pre-incarnate glory to take on human form—and the form of a servant, no less? He had a mission to accomplish. The reason Jesus left the glory and majesty of being at the right hand of the Father in heaven was His focus on the interests of others. He offered the most precious sacrifice when "he humbled himself by becoming obedient to the point of death, even death on the cross" (Phil. 2:8).

While it is the most natural thing to focus on your own problems during unemployment, you find freedom from self-absorption by serving others.

The cross stands as the epitome of what it means to count others as significant and to look to the interests of others. This is why the cross is the perfect depiction of true humility. The proud will never show this type of self-abnegation and self-denial. The human heart is self-sufficient, self-reliant, self-exalting and self-focused, always demanding its rights and privileges. Humans will manipulate or dominate in order to get what they believe they "rightfully" deserve.

While it is the most natural thing to focus on your own problems during unemployment, you find freedom from self-absorption by serving others. There are no simple solutions, no quick steps to take, but with time, persistence and the grace of God, you can move from pride to humility.

Dismantling Pride

I am sure we all know people who feverishly fought to gain a position, ruthlessly crushing whoever was in the way. We could identify individuals who have ignored the needs of others to maintain their standard of living. But the real challenge comes with a look in the mirror. Where have I been guilty of pride? In what do I boast?

The journey of unemployment took me down some hideous paths. God exposed the grotesqueness of my pride and arrogance. There were times I wished this trial on others or cried out that it was unfair. I thought I "deserved" better treatment than this. I even found myself comparing myself to others. Shame on me for such self-promotion and self-exaltation!

The longer I remained unemployed the more the Lord began to dismantle these thought patterns. Slowly the remnants of self-reliance and self-sufficiency were torn down. God stripped them away one layer at a time, then opened my eyes to see the altar of self-idolatry I had erected.

I needed to come to the point of recognizing my utter dependence on the Lord and to see every ability, talent and accomplishment as a gift from heaven. To do otherwise is to ascribe glory to myself.

The humility of John the Baptist was seen in what he said of Christ: "He must increase, but I must decrease" (John 3:30). Anything that promotes self is proclaiming, "I must increase." To pray for Christ to increase in our life is also to pray for self to diminish. In other words, we must deny ourselves, take up our cross and follow Christ (Luke 9:23). A prayer entitled "God's Cause" puts it this way:

Lord, use me as Thou wilt,
do with me what Thou wilt;
but, O, promote Thy cause,
let Thy kingdom come,
let Thy blessed interest
be advanced in this world![3]

Many times I have thought, "Lord, I have served You for so many years. Why won't You give me what I want?" That was the problem. I was more concerned about what I wanted than what He wanted. If the cry of my heart is to say, "Thy cause, not my own,"[4] and my desire is to be used of God for the greatest advancement of the Kingdom, will I be willing to be used in the ways He wills and allow Him to do with me whatever He desires? What if it is God's will for us to shine as lights in the midst of unemployment? Will we be willing to say, "Lord, use me as You will, but promote Your cause"? What if the way our Father in heaven wants to use us is to show the world that His people can live well—live a life which honors and glorifies Him—with or without work? Would we still say, "Father, let Your blessed interest be advanced in this world!" To live well is to be consumed with God's cause, and not my own.

Disciplines for Growing in Humility

C.J. Mahaney stated, "The crucial question is not whether we will suffer, but how we'll respond when we suffer."[5] Suffering through joblessness in a God-honoring way means we must begin each day acknowledging our dependence on God. How do we do this? Three practices we can engage in are specified by Mahaney in his book, *Humility: True Greatness*.

1. Meditating on the Cross and the Gospel

Meditating on the cross is a way to preach the gospel to ourselves every day. "The cross never flatters us,"[6] Mahaney says; meditating on Christ's sacrifice helps us recognize our sin and wretchedness, and the depths of rebellion in our hearts. It causes us to confess our pride and arrogance, and realize the foolish ways in which we once walked—in rebellion, deceit, bitterness and violence (Rom. 3:10–18).

Meditating on the cross also focuses our thoughts on the atonement Christ accomplished through His humble obedience to the point of death. It causes us to worship and thank the Father that we have been justified, and reminds us that there is nothing which we can boast in other than Christ alone. Justification is not based on any work of man, but by the grace of God which is "poured out on us richly through Jesus Christ our Savior" (Titus 3:4–7).

To meditate on the atonement is to praise God for the redemption of all whom the Father has called. It reminds us that we were liberated from slavery to sin. Redemption points to our freedom which was "bought with a price" (1 Cor. 6:20). The price Christ paid was that he "redeemed us from the curse of the law by becoming a curse for us" (Gal. 3:13). True humility grows in us as we remember that there is nothing we were able to do to gain freedom from sin's enslavement.

2. Meditating on the Attributes of God

Another key discipline is to study the Scriptures to see the greatness and holiness of God. It can be especially helpful to study the attributes of God, especially those known as *incommunicable*—possessed by God alone.[7] This includes such attributes such as infinitude, omnipresence, self-existence and self-sufficiency. Mahaney notes that a study on the character of God stomps down pride because "we become increasingly aware of the indescribably vast distance between ourselves and God."[8]

There are many sources one can use to begin a study on the attributes of God. I strongly recommend reading *Knowing God* by J.I. Packer, *The Holiness of God* by R.C. Sproul, and *The Sovereignty of God* by Arthur W. Pink. Each of these works nurtures an understanding of the greatness of God. It also exposes the unworthiness of man which is a sure-fire way of dismantling pride and growing in humility.

The only way to get a divine perspective on job loss is to set our eyes on the greatness and goodness of God, and remember that His purposes are never thwarted.

Nothing, however, can replace *reading Scripture* for insight into God's nature. The book of Job is a good place to begin to learn about humility. No length of time in unemployment can equal the extent of the suffering and hardship in which Job endured. Job was a righteous man and innocent of the accusations thrown at him by his so-called friends. And yet, as the book progresses, a subtle spiritual pride tends to seep out of Job's responses. Ben Patterson observes, "He defends his cause at the expense of God's good name. He sets himself up as the judge of the Judge, the god of God, and in effect accuses God of doing evil!"[9]

In answering Job God never directly addresses the questions he raised. Instead, through an intense interrogation,

God shatters his pride (Job 38–41). There is only one response Job is able to give after being confronted with the reality of the greatness, awesomeness and majesty of the Sovereign Lord of the universe:

> I know that you can do all things, and that no purpose of yours can be thwarted. . . . I have uttered what I did not understand, things too wonderful for me, which I did not know. . . . I have heard of you by the hearing of the ear, but now my eye sees you; therefore I despise myself, and repent in dust and ashes. (Job 42:3–6)

To battle the ever-present pride in one's heart, there must be a concerted effort to attack it at its roots. The more we come to see the greatness of God, Mahaney says, the more we will gain a "divine perspective of perplexing and troubling circumstances."[10] The only way to get a divine perspective on job loss is to set our eyes on the greatness and goodness of God, and remember that His purposes are never thwarted.

3. Engaging in Service to Others

Mahaney also observes that "Only the humble are genuinely concerned about edifying and encouraging others."[11] The other side to this truth is that edifying and encouraging others helps us grow in humility. Trials can make us inwardly focused; self-pity and a "woe is me" spirit develops. The more we focus on ministering to others and praying for their needs, the less we dwell on our own problems, and the less stress and anxiety we experience.

The battle against pride is never-ending, and we must declare war on all its manifestations, including self-centeredness. Look for practical ways to serve and encourage others.

Put some effort into identifying those with needs, and learn how you can help. Prepare your heart and mind and suit up for battle (Eph. 6:10–20).

Take a break from filling out applications and write some notes of encouragement. If you face a particularly hard day in the job search, take a respite and go visit someone who is sick or hospitalized. When you can't get your mind off the endless cycle of "what if I can't find a job" scenarios, make it a point to pray for or with someone who is hurting and struggling with life's issues. This is what it means to live the God-honoring life even in the midst of unemployment. It is letting God do His work to mold you into the likeness of Christ. It is to nurture an others-centered perspective.

Chapter Four

Growing in Contentment

The stress of joblessness affects a person physically, not just emotionally. Before unemployment I never had problems sleeping at night. Since I have been out of work, however, getting a good night's rest has become much more of a challenge. I often found myself staring at the ceiling in the middle of the night, the minutes and hours just ticking away.

What was it that kept me up? Worry. Where will we get the money for the mortgage payment? How much will the utility bills be this month, and where will we get the money to pay them? I can remember many nights crying and wondering, "Lord, are we going to lose everything?" Worry creates stress, stress causes anxiety, and anxiety produces nothing of value. Knowing all this did not relieve the financial burdens. Eventually I began to complain and grumble about the lot in life which I had been given. It all seemed unfair.

Grumbling seems to be the chief response of the people of Israel in the wilderness after crossing the Red Sea. On three different occasions the nation of Israel grumbled and doubted God's provision. Exodus 14 recalls how they doubted God would fulfill His promise of deliverance from Egypt and complained to Moses saying, "Is it because there are no graves in Egypt that you have taken us away to die in the wilderness? What have you done to us in bringing us out of Egypt?" (14:12). Exodus 15 tells how the people grumbled and complained the water was not fit to drink (15:24). Exodus 16 recounts how

> . . . the whole congregation of the people of Israel grumbled against Moses and Aaron in the wilderness, and the people of Israel said to them, "Would that we had died by the hand of the LORD in the land of Egypt, when we sat by the meat pots and ate bread to the full, for you have brought us out into this wilderness to kill this whole assembly with hunger." (2–3)

It is easy to say, "I can't believe these people! What was their problem? They had just seen God miraculously deliver them through the plagues in Egypt and the parting of the Red Sea. If God can do all this, isn't He more than able to supply their need for water and food? Did they seriously think that God would not provide fresh water and bread to eat?" And yet, when I found myself in a similar tight spot, what did I do? I grumbled.

Grumbling stems from a lack of faith. It is doubting His ways and questioning His wisdom, doubting His faithfulness and questioning His promises, doubting His goodness and questioning His love and mercy. Are we not just as guilty of unbelief when we are in the valleys of life?

Unemployment leaves a person in a precarious position.

When we don't know when or from where our income is coming, we are forced to depend on the Lord in ways we never have before. Before being out of work, I did not fully appreciate the prayer, "Give us this day our daily bread" (Matt. 6:11). It implies walking by faith one day at a time. This is why the journey teaches us the God-honoring attitude of humility.

> *Covetousness encompasses more than just material possessions. It includes any longing and craving for something we do not have.*

Since unemployment confronts us with our limitations and frailty, we can slip into grumbling about our circumstances and be consumed with self-pity. Just as the Israelites complained about losing what they had back in the "good old days" in Egypt, we are apt to complain about losing our position and the "good old days" we used to enjoy. Grumble, grumble, grumble.

The Assassin of Contentment

We grumble because we are discontented and dissatisfied with our position in life. This lack of contentment is often fueled by the sin of covetousness (Exod. 20:17; Deut. 5:21). Paul equates covetousness with idolatry (Col. 3:5) and warns that those who covet will have "no inheritance in the kingdom of Christ and God" (Eph. 5:5).

What does it mean to covet? James MacDonald defined covetousness as "wanting wrong things, or wanting right things for the wrong reasons, or at the wrong time, or in the wrong amount."[1] This broad definition encompasses more than just material possessions. It includes any longing and craving for something we do not have. It leads to discontentment, selfishness and self-centeredness; if we can't acquire it, we grumble and complain because we feel we deserve it.

The Snare of Covetousness

After providing a sensational victory over the well-fortified city of Jericho (Josh. 6), God allowed the nation of Israel to face a devastating defeat at Ai because there was sin in the camp (7:1–12). Achan confessed he was the guilty party:

> Truly I have sinned against the Lord God of Israel and this is what I did: When I *saw* among the spoil a beautiful cloak from Shinar, and 200 shekels of silver, and a bar of gold weighing 50 shekels, then I *coveted* them and *took* them. And see, they are hidden in the earth inside my tent, with the silver underneath. (7:20–21)

This confession reveals the progressive nature of covetousness. The first step is looking; the text says Achan "saw." This was not just a passing glance; it was an intentional and deliberate examination, and you can tell that by the way he described the items. It wasn't just a cloak; it was a "beautiful cloak from Shinar." He must have held it and examined the fabric and manner in which it was made to identify it as being from Shinar. In the same way, today you might notice a man's suit, but only after closer examination could you determine it was an Armani, worth over $2,000. His description of the other items was similarly detailed: he knew the exact number of shekels of silver and the precise weight of the gold bar. The first step in covetousness is always the snare of taking an extended look. Lusting after something which does not belong to you leads to ruin.

The next step is desire and longing. After examining the items, Achan "coveted." The more he looked, the more attractive they became. The more attractive they appeared, the more he delighted in them and wanted them. I can just imagine Achan taking the cloak in his hands, possibly even trying it on. The more he handled it the more he treasured it in his heart. Eventually he came to the point where he said, "I've just got to have this." Finally, Achan took the items. Matthew Henry said "it was not the looking, but the lusting that ruined him."[2] This is always the nature of covetousness.

The account of the Fall follows the same three steps. First, Eve "*saw* that the tree was good for food." Then Eve coveted, finding the fruit attractive because it "was a delight to the eyes and that the tree was to be desired to make one wise." Finally, Eve committed the sin and ate (Gen. 3:6).

David's sin with Bathsheba also follows the same pattern. David *saw*: "It happened, late one afternoon, when David arose from his couch and was walking on the roof of the king's house, that *he saw* from the roof a woman bathing." Then David *coveted*. He found her to be attractive and "very beautiful." It was not a passing glance, but rather he went on to "inquire about the woman." Then David *took*. He sent messengers and "took her, and she came to him, and he lay with her" (2 Sam. 11:1–4).

A Universal Problem

Covetousness is deeply rooted in the human heart. Jesus adamantly warned, "Take care, and be on your guard against all covetousness, for one's life does not consist in the abundance of his possessions" (Luke 12:15). Achan coveted fine clothes and money. Eve coveted fruit of the tree of the knowledge of good and evil. David coveted a beautiful woman. There is no end to the things we covet. Regardless of the form it takes, covetousness always saps our spiritual life. If we want to live a Christ-centered life, we must put it to death (Col. 3:5). In the process we gain the blessing of contentment.

If covetousness is either longing for the *wrong* things, or the *right* things in the *wrong* way, then it stands to reason that it is possible to want the *right* things in the *right* way. In other words, not all passions and longings are necessarily covetousness. Righteousness is not the denial of all passion, but the channeling of right passions in the right direction. Only when the longing for a person, treasure or thing becomes more valuable than Christ do we begin to covet.

Covetousness is not easy to detect. We dress sin up so it looks nicer than it is; we label it with new names so that it doesn't sound so bad. We suppress the truth and are quick to exchange the glory of God for artificial and superficial replacements like material possessions and other objects (Rom. 1:18–25). But God makes it abundantly clear that if we treasure anything above Him, it is idolatry.

Covetousness is universal. It has no socio-economic limitations; from the wealthy in upscale neighborhoods to the middle class sprawled out in suburbia to the poor in urban slums, it reaches its tentacles into every segment of society. Covetousness is not an issue of one's income, standard of living, age, nationality or ethnicity; we all struggle with the insatiable longing for better, for newer or simply for more. Covetousness is an equal opportunity destroyer.

You are likely to find yourself more tempted to covetousness when you are out of work. Typically, however, it takes the form of a desperate desire to keep from losing what you already have, rather than a desire to obtain what you don't have. This is the challenge in unemployment. Joblessness can also be a time when we wrestle with wanting right things, but in the wrong time. When a job offer falls through, do we grumble? Do we complain if the job God provides is not the one we wanted? Is this what God wants from His people? Does this attitude bring glory to His name?

Defining Biblical Contentment

The American marketing industry is a multi-billion dollar enterprise with one simple objective: to make us feel we "just gotta have" whatever it is they are selling. The marketing industry is built on fostering discontent and covetousness. From cars to cell phones to clothing to cologne—everything is now a "necessity." When we are not able to obtain them, we grumble and complain, dissatisfied with our lot in life. Living well involves seeing the great gain in contentment and learning its secret.

Pursue Great Gain

Paul expresses this godly attitude near the end of his first letter to Timothy: "Now there is great gain in godliness with contentment, for we brought nothing into the world, and we cannot take anything out of this world. But if we have food and clothing, with these we will be content" (6:6–8).

It is no coincidence that this passage is bookended by two warnings, one against false teachers driven by a desire for financial prosperity (6:3–5) and the other against the pursuit of wealth—a snare which can lead to ruin (6:9–10). In the middle of these two warnings against the pursuit of wealth is the exhortation to pursue the true wealth: godliness with contentment. This text provides three essential concepts for developing a heart of contentment.

1. Biblical contentment is spiritually enriching. Many engage in a desperate pursuit of wealth, believing it will provide happiness. But as Steve Lawson has aptly remarked, "Happiness is not a goal, it is always a by-product."[3] The paradox is this: those who make happiness the goal are often the most miserable. Pursuing riches to gain happiness simply does not work. Covetousness is never the path to true joy. So why do so many set their sights on the world's treasures and say, "If only I had a particular income level, then I would be happy; if only I owned this, then I would be content"?

When we make the glory of God the central goal of our lives, genuine happiness naturally follows.

Conversely, when we make the glory of God the central goal of our lives, genuine happiness naturally follows. If contentment is being fully satisfied, then "godliness with contentment" (1 Tim. 6:6) is being fully satisfied in God, regardless of one's economic status.

For many Christians godliness with contentment seems elusive. Though we might say we desire to grow in Christlikeness, we also want satisfaction with wealth and material possessions. We wrestle with covetousness. We desire God; but we also long to have gold. We long to know Jesus; but we also treasure jewels. As long as we attempt to pursue two masters, we will never experience contentment. As long as there is the insatiable appetite for the treasures of this world, we have not yet come to the point where we can say we count "everything as loss because of the surpassing worth of knowing Christ Jesus [our] Lord" (Phil. 3:8). The Christ-centered life rings out, "In the morning when I rise, give me Jesus. . . . When I am alone, give me Jesus. . . . You can have all this world, just give me Jesus."[4] This is the heart of godliness and contentment. This is great gain. This is living well. This we can do with or without work.

2. Biblical contentment is eternally focused. Paul declares, "We brought nothing into the world, and we cannot take anything out of the world" (1 Tim. 6:7). After Job lost all his earthly possessions, his family and his health, he proclaimed, "Naked I came from my mother's womb, and naked shall I return. The LORD gave, and the LORD has taken away; blessed be the name of the LORD" (Job 1:21).

Contentment arises from an eternal perspective. It develops when our focus is upon our eternal inheritance. This world is temporal and will pass away. To know the world will be burned up and dissolved—along with all its riches—ought to make us pursue the one true treasure worth possessing: Jesus Christ. The Christ-centered life is being satisfied in our union and fellowship with Christ and pursuing a life which reflects Him—a life of holiness and godliness (2 Pet. 3:10–11).

3. Biblical contentment is need-based. Paul goes on to say that all we need to be content is "food and covering" (1 Tim. 6:8). Would we be content with basic nourishment—no expensive dinners or tasty snacks? Or would we be like the Israelites, who complained and grumbled over the manna from heaven? Would we be satisfied with mere "covering"—basic provisions to cover our nakedness and to protect us from the elements? This is humbling to consider. I have never reached the point where all I had to eat was bread and water.

So why do we fret and worry? Why do we continue to stress out about what we have? It is because we are not content; we always long for more. There is such a pull to get what we don't have and keep what we do have. To do without is viewed as failure. If we are going to experience contentment we must be satisfied with basic needs. When we focus on the things of this world, we lose our contentment and grumbling sets in.

We live in an affluent society and face a daily battle over which master we will serve. Will it be God or money? Will I find complete satisfaction in the surpassing worth of knowing Christ, or will I look for satisfaction in the fleeting enjoyments which come from temporal pleasures? The Christ-centered life is having satisfaction in the basic needs while treasuring Christ above all.

Learn the Great Secret

Writing to the Philippians, Paul shares the secret to living the Christ-centered life of contentment:

> Not that I am speaking of being in need, for I have learned in whatever situation I am to be content. I know how to be brought low, and I know how to abound. In any and every circumstance, I have learned the secret of facing plenty and hunger, abundance and need. I can do all things through him who strengthens me. (Phil. 4:11–13)

What is the secret to contentment? It is where we place our trust and dependence. Paul knew how to live well—in poverty or prosperity. Which is easier? We might think it is easier to be content with prosperity, but this isn't even the right question. We can be discontent in abundance as well as when we have need. The key to living well has nothing to do with our socio-economic level. If Paul had been asked this question, I believe he would have responded that the secret to being satisfied—whether rich or poor—is literally and figuratively out of this world. The secret is not a principle to follow; it is a Person to trust. The secret is "I can do all things through Him who strengthens me" (Phil. 4:13). Therefore, the right question to ask is, who are you trusting?

Do we trust in Jesus or our finances? Do we treasure Christ alone or do we also treasure our material possessions? Do we really trust God's grace to be sufficient to meet all our needs? Don't be quick to skip over these questions, because the true answer to them is reflected in the way we live our lives.

Joblessness has repeatedly taken me to the brink, forcing me to choose between living in contentment and satisfaction by the sufficiency of God's grace, or slipping into the downward spiral of discontentment. We are pressured to conform to the pattern of this world and succumb to the tantalizing lure of its attractions and possessions—and the deck is stacked against us. We live in world that entices us to dissatisfaction; the struggle only intensifies during unemployment. Can we remain content even if God chooses to take what we have away? Will we be able to say, "the LORD gave, and the LORD has taken away; blessed be the name of the LORD" (Job 1:21)?

Trusting in Christ's Sufficiency

God graciously saved the Israelites from bondage in Egypt, yet in His infinite and matchless power, He delivers all whom He has chosen from the bondage of sin and the domain of darkness and transfers us into the kingdom of His Son (Col. 1:13). Jesus Christ won the victory over sin and death through the redemption He secured by His sacrificial death on the cross. He offered Himself as the perfect Lamb to forgive my sins and cancel the debt I could not pay. So is there anything too hard for our God?

To our shame, we are just like the Israelites in the wilderness, who worried about food and water even after the Lord delivered them from slavery (Exod. 14–16). We worry and fret over basic provisions even after the Lord delivered us from the domain of darkness. Nothing has changed. To experience contentment requires trusting in the sufficiency of the grace of God.

Unemployment is a hard place to be. It is a difficult and painful road to travel. It is easy to complain. But to grumble against circumstances is actually to grumble against the Lord. "The LORD has heard your grumbling that you grumble against Him . . . your grumbling is not against us, but against the LORD" (Exod. 16:8). It is defiantly saying, "Is the LORD among us or not?" (Exod. 17:7). Grumbling is an affront to His sovereignty and an offense against His infinite wisdom. It is an injustice against His matchless love and grace. The only way to live well is to put your full trust in Christ.

Disciplines for Growing in Contentment

We are not talking about a one-time skirmish, but a life-long battle. When the hardships increase and the sacrifices cut deeper, our flesh will buffet us with thoughts of dissatisfaction. This will lead to anxiety and grumbling. This is why it is important for us to preach the gospel to ourselves every day. The Christ-centered life is a contented life. It is finding complete satisfaction in the sufficiency and goodness of the Lord.

The Christ-centered life is a contented life. It is finding complete satisfaction in the sufficiency and goodness of the Lord.

The battle for contentment is a battle for the mind. Whether gainfully employed or living without work, we struggle with discontentment because our hearts and minds are corrupt. The battle is centered on whom we trust and serve. We can only serve one master: "either [we] will love the one and hate the other, or [we] will be devoted to the one and despise the other" (Matt. 6:24). We will either store up treasures on earth which will fade away or store up treasure in heaven which is imperishable (Matt. 6:19–20). So what is the battle plan for attacking discontentment? What path do we need to travel to live the Christ-centered life of contentment, regardless of life's circumstances?

First of all, we must understand that we cannot do this in our own strength. It is the Holy Spirit who enables and empowers us with the spiritual resources to fight the battle. When Paul wrote, "I can do all things through him who strengthens me" (Phil. 4:13), he was speaking specifically of learning to be content.

Contentment comes by abiding in fellowship with Christ. The more we are satisfied in our fellowship with Christ the more we will be content. Therefore, waging war against dissatisfaction and the snare of covetousness flows from trusting and clinging to the promises of God. There are five promises which will be helpful in this battle. I encourage you to memorize them.

Promise 1: God Is Working Out All Things for Good

"And we know that for those who love God all things work together for good, for those who are called according to his purpose" (Rom. 8:28). This verse is often taken out of context. In our context the "good" is not a good-paying job. In fact, the "good" has nothing to do with material and temporal things such as employment, income or possessions. We must see the "good" from a Christ-centered perspective. The "good" is being conformed to the image of Jesus Christ (Rom. 8:29). Therefore the "good" is spiritual; not material. The "good" is eternal, not temporal. In this regard even trials and hardships can be good. By His grace, God works in and through trials such as unemployment for our good and as a means of conforming us more into the likeness of His Son. In the light of this truth, we can view joblessness as the fertile soil to mature us in the Christ-centered life.

Promise 2: God Knows What You Need before You Ask

Matthew 6:25–34 records Jesus preaching on the issue of worry and anxiety. After drawing attention to how God provides abundantly for the birds of the air and the lilies of the field, the Lord speaks specifically in verses 31 to 33 on the issue of contentment:

Therefore do not be anxious, saying "What shall we eat?" or "What shall we drink?" or "What shall we wear?" for the Gentiles seek after these things, and your heavenly Father knows that you need them all. But seek first the kingdom of God and his righteousness, and all these things will be added to you.

When our focus is skewed and set upon the treasures of this world—home, food, clothing, occupation—anxiety and worry mounts. Jesus rebukes this. The way to counter worry and anxiety is to remember the sovereignty and goodness of God in the way He abundantly provides for His creation. If God cares enough to provide for birds and flowers, can we not trust Him to be faithful to provide for us as well?

Jesus concludes this section of the Sermon on the Mount by stating that the way to turn worry into contentment and anxiety into satisfaction is to focus on Christ and His kingdom. Cling to the promise that God knows what we need even before we ask Him, and that He is caring and good in providing for His creation.

Promise 3: God Will Supply Every Need According to His Riches in Glory in Christ Jesus

The Philippian church was very generous and sacrificial in their giving, even though they themselves had great need (2 Cor. 8:1–4). Paul appreciated their generosity and encouraged them with this promise: "And my God will supply every need of yours according to his riches in glory in Christ Jesus" (Phil. 4:19).

The knee-jerk reaction when finances are a struggle is to become tight-fisted and hoard our resources. We work to keep the bank account as large as possible; we are reluctant to give to others. Yet the Bible stresses that "whoever sows sparingly will also reap sparingly, and whoever sows bountifully will also reap bountifully" (2 Cor. 9:6). Even during difficult financial times we are called to be cheerful givers, and to remember that no one can give more than God can supply (2 Cor. 9:8).

God wants us to live in complete dependence on Him so that we may truly experience the riches of His grace, goodness and glory.

The blessing of this promise goes much deeper than mere financial need. It states that God will supply our every need according to the *riches of His glory*. God wants us to live in complete dependence on Him so that we may truly experience the riches of His grace, goodness and glory. Sometimes He requires us to make deep sacrifices and endure very troubling times. But we can cling to the promise that in all things, our God will supply every need according to His riches in glory in Christ Jesus.

Promise 4: God Will Strengthen and Help Me in My Time of Need

It is easy to allow the harshness of unemployment to seize up our spiritual life. It can create fear which binds up our hearts. What truth can free us from this fear? "Fear not, for I am with you; be not dismayed, for I am your God; I will strengthen you, I will help you, I will uphold you with my righteous right hand" (Isa. 41:10).

Isaiah was prophetically warning of impending disaster.

God reassured His people that even if they went through national calamities, "Fear not, I am with you." Jesus spoke similar words to His disciples, saying, "Behold, I am with you always, to the end of the age" (Matt. 28:20).

God has promised to be with us at all times, until the end of time. God has promised to strengthen us through His Spirit so that we remain steadfast and persevere until the end. So when anxiety begins to mount, remember: Fear not, for the Lord your God is with you! He may not remove the trial, but He will strengthen and help you. He may not lessen the hardship, but He will be there with you in the midst of it to carry you through.

Promise 5: The Grace of God Is Sufficient in My Weakness

If you get a splinter in your finger, what is your first response? You want to remove it—the pain drives you to do whatever it takes to get it out. The same is true with trials. The natural and immediate response is to try to get out from under the trial. But is this always best? Paul received a "thorn in the flesh"; we don't know exactly what he was referring to, but just like a splinter, he wanted to get rid of it. He prayed to the Lord three times to have it removed. God's response was, "My grace is sufficient for you, for my power is made perfect in weakness" (2 Cor. 12:9).

The blessing of trials is that they bring us to a point of deeper trust, reliance and dependence on Christ, through the aid of the Holy Spirit. Just like Paul's thorn, unemployment can be a wonderful opportunity for the power of Christ to be displayed in our lives. When we allow this to happen, our contentment and satisfaction in the grace of God overcomes our anxiety and provides real peace. This is truly a precious jewel.

Chapter Five

Growing in Joy

Long-term unemployment can be very discouraging, and even lead to depression. There are days when it is a struggle just to get out of bed. As the days turn into weeks, and the weeks into months with no apparent progress, it feels like being at the bottom of a thirty-foot pit with the walls caving in. The hope of finding employment becomes dimmer the longer one remains out of work. Negative news reports on the sluggish economy and the bleak outlook for the future only sinks the jobless person even deeper into an emotional quagmire.

After nearly six months of being unemployed and going through the same routine every day—diligently conducting a job search but getting no results—I felt like giving up. It seemed like an unrealistic and hopeless endeavor. Then I remembered the words to that old hymn:

> Have we trials and temptations?
> Is there trouble anywhere?
> We should never be discouraged,
> Take it to the Lord in prayer.[1]

Really? We should *never* be discouraged? How can we *never* be discouraged when it seems as if the weight of the world is upon us? There have been many days when I felt I was bordering on depression.

It is possible, of course, to suffer from depression because of a physiological ailment, but for the vast majority of us, discouragement and depression are rooted in emotional and spiritual issues. Imagine a beautiful flower garden in full bloom. The setting is tranquil and restful; it has the power to lift our spirits and boost our emotional state. What happens, though, if we do not properly care for the garden? It won't be long before it becomes overrun with weeds and thistles. Something of great beauty turns into an eyesore, and instead of boosting our spirits, it fills us with gloom.

One particular sinful attitude which becomes evident in joblessness is cynicism—the tendency to emphasize the negative, to expect the worst, to take a jaded perspective on life.

It is the same with the condition of our souls. At conversion we become a new creation (2 Cor. 5:17), and the Holy Spirit implants new life within us (John 6:63). Through regeneration our souls which were once dead in sin are now made alive to God (Eph. 2:1). When we walk by the Spirit, the spiritual garden of our new life in Christ grows and blossoms as we bear the fruit of the Spirit (Gal. 5:16–23).

But conversion does not eradicate the sin nature. The power of sin is broken but its presence remains. We must work out our salvation with fear and trembling (Phil. 2:12).

If not, the garden of our new life in Christ becomes overrun with the weeds and thistles of sinful attitudes, deeds and words.

One particular sinful attitude which becomes evident in joblessness is cynicism—the tendency to emphasize the negative, to expect the worst, to take a jaded perspective on life. If this attitude is not weeded out, discouragement and despair will spread and choke out the fruit of the Spirit, which includes joy. John Piper notes that the loss of joy has plagued many leaders in the history of the church:

> Virtually all Bible-saturated physicians of the soul have spoken about long seasons of darkness and desolation. In the old days they called it melancholy. . . . It happens because of sin, or because of Satanic assault, or because of distressing circumstances, or because of hereditary or other physical causes.[2]

Today, "seasons of darkness" and "melancholy" would most likely be diagnosed as depression. Unemployment is one of the "distressing circumstances" which can trigger this depression. This is why we must deal with the cynicism which arises during these times. It is one thing to prevent depression but another thing to have joy. How do we nurture joy in distressing times, such as when we're without work?

Defining Biblical Joy

Piper sees Christian joy as something we have to fight to maintain in our lives. We can win the battle if we keep the perspective that "all that God is for us in Jesus is the Object of our quest for joy."[3] The fight for joy when we are hard-pressed is not a fight to find joy *in* the suffering, but to have joy in the Lord *in the midst of* the suffering. Joy is always linked with an object.

Many attempt to make a distinction between joy and happiness, but there is no clear difference between the two words in Scripture. What people usually mean when they contrast joy and happiness is the distinction between a biblical and a worldly view of joy.

The primary thing that distinguishes biblical joy from worldly joy is its source or object. Worldly happiness has its object in circumstances. It is something temporal, such as a job, possessions or a relationship. Worldly happiness only lasts until the circumstances change; when the source of our joy disappears, our happiness also vanishes. If prosperity is the object of our happiness, the loss of a job and the downturn in finances causes happiness to disappear, and depression sets in. This focus on the wrong object is what needs to be pulled out by the roots if the spiritual garden of our soul is to flourish and bear much fruit.

The Scriptures declare that the object of true joy is Christ, and since Christ is eternal and will never diminish in value and worth, our joy in Him will never diminish over time. In fact, the more we grow in intimate fellowship with Christ, the more our joy will increase, regardless of the circumstances of our life.

This concept sounds good in theory, but how do we apply it in real life? Let's take a look at some concrete, biblical examples we can imitate.

David: The Rejoicing Fugitive

Samuel anointed David to be the new king of Israel after

Saul had sinned against the Lord (1 Sam. 16). It was many years, however, before David was able to assume the throne. In the interim Saul tried to assassinate David several times (chaps. 18–19). David's safety was so much in jeopardy that he was forced to flee and hide in the hill country as a fugitive (chaps. 20–22).

David certainly had no cause for joy based on his circumstances! If anyone had a right to slip into depression and despair, it was David. Yet this is not the testimony of Scripture. During the same period he was on the run as a fugitive, David wrote some of the most moving expressions of joy and praise recorded in the book of Psalms. He remained joyful because the object of his joy was not his circumstances. The gladness of his heart overflowed from his delight in the Rock of his salvation (Ps. 31:1–2). David's gladness did not waver because his trust was in an unwavering source: "Blessed is the man who makes the LORD his trust" (Ps. 40:4). David was a rejoicing fugitive because of his confidence in the promises of God:

> Though I walk in the midst of trouble,
>   you preserve my life;
> you stretch out your hand against the wrath of my enemies,
>   and your right hand delivers me.
> The LORD will fulfill his purpose for me;
>   your steadfast love, O LORD, endures forever.
> Do not forsake the work of your hands. (Ps. 138:7–8)

The object of David's joy was the nature and character of the Lord. When we become depressed, it is often because we have not removed the weeds which have grown up in our heart and mind, and have taken our focus off Christ alone. But if we, like David, keep our focus and remain joyful through tough times like joblessness, our light will shine before men.

Paul and Silas: The Rejoicing Prisoners

Paul is another example of one who kept Christ as the object and quest of his joy. He and Silas were beaten and thrown into jail while proclaiming the gospel in Philippi. Had their happiness stemmed from their circumstances, we might expect them to wallow in self-pity as they sat in chains: "Lord, we don't understand. We were doing Your will. Yet look at us now—bruised and beaten! Why, Lord?"

Discouragement mounts and depression deepens the more we focus on our circumstances. Paul chose a different path. He responded by "praying and singing hymns to God" (Acts 16:25).

Does this refrain sound familiar? We are all prone to self-pity when things don't go the way we think they should. Discouragement mounts and depression deepens the more we focus on our circumstances. Paul chose a different path. He responded by "praying and singing hymns to God" (Acts 16:25). How was he able to do this, and how can we have this same joyful resolve? Paul's secret was the object of his joy. It was his confidence in Christ: "I know whom I have believed, and I am convinced that he is able to guard until that Day what has been entrusted to me" (2 Tim. 1:12).

Spiritual Myopia

Myopia, more commonly known as near-sightedness, is a condition of the eye where objects up close are clearly seen, but objects in the distance are blurred. The same condition can be true of our spiritual sight. Immediate circumstances of life can be seen clearly, but the reality of what lies beyond this world is blurred. In order to have joy in life, we need to correct our spiritual vision.

> Therefore, since we are surrounded by so great a cloud of witnesses, let us also lay aside every weight, and sin which clings so closely, and let us run with endurance the race that is set before us, looking to Jesus, the founder and perfecter of our faith, who for the joy that was set before him endured the cross, despising the shame, and is seated at the right hand of the throne of God. (Heb. 12:1–2)

What was the joy set before Jesus? His joy was centered on something beyond the suffering of the cross. It was focused upon His eternal reward and inheritance. His sight was on the day when He would again be seated at the right hand of the throne of God.

To correct spiritual myopia, our vision must be eternally focused. We must keep our eyes on the hope of our promised inheritance (Heb. 9:15; 1 Pet. 1:4), on the outcome of our faith—the salvation of our souls (1 Pet. 1:9), on the promise of dwelling in the house of the Lord forever (Ps. 23:6). We must focus our sight on the glorious day when God "will wipe away every tear from [our] eyes, and death shall be no more, neither shall there be mourning, nor crying, nor pain anymore, for the former things have passed away" (Rev. 21:4). This eternal perspective will radically change the way we react and respond to the trials of life, because they will be put into proper perspective.

The apostle Paul had correct spiritual vision. Even though he went through many trials, he always kept his focus on the treasure of "the knowledge of the glory of God in the face of Jesus Christ" (2 Cor. 4:6). When he was afflicted, he was not crushed; when he was perplexed, he was not driven to a point of utter despair. He did not lose heart because his joy was in Christ. He did not sink into depression because his spiritual sight was focused on that which is eternal:

> So we do not lose heart. Though our outer self is wasting away, our inner self is being renewed day by day. For this light momentary affliction is preparing for us an eternal weight of glory beyond all comparison, as we look not to the things that are seen but to the things that are unseen. For the things that are seen are transient, but the things that are unseen are eternal. (2 Cor. 4:14–18)

Unemployment is by no means the worst trial we are likely to endure in this life—and certainly not as difficult as the hardships many fellow Christians around the world face every day. Throughout the history of the church, many believers have suffered intense persecution for their faith. The key to their perseverance was keeping everything in perspective—seeing the eternal weight of glory as being far beyond comparison to the temporal afflictions of this life.

The book of Revelation was written to give hope to suffering Christians. John, the author, draws our vision to the incomparable glory of Jesus Christ (1:12–18), especially the glory of Christ as Lord of the church (2:1–3:22). The climax of the revelation is the vision of seeing and delighting in the glory of God in the face of Jesus Christ, which results in on-going, joyful worship around the throne of God (4:1–5:14).

The vision of "the things that must soon take place" (1:1) corrects our spiritual sight, because it focuses on the object of our joy—the glory of the risen Lord. Our sight is also corrected when we take in the glory of Christ in His righteous judgments (6:1–20:15). The picture is completed as our eyes are drawn to the glory of Christ in the eternal state when "the dwelling place of God is with man. He will dwell with them, and they will be his people and God himself will be with them as their God" (21:3). Jesus Christ is our hope. Jesus Christ is the object of our joy.

If we settle for that which is seen and temporal, we continually struggle to keep our worship and joy from shriveling up.

With this vision of Christ given in Revelation, what could possibly steal our joy? Yet the challenges of life often appear so insurmountable that they block out this glorious vision. Every negative news report on the economy, every bill or rejection letter in the mail, only strengthens our spiritual myopia. Then we become discouraged and our short-sightedness robs us of our joy.

Piper points out that this loss of a far-reaching vision affects not only our joy, but even our capacity for worship:

> The enemy of worship is not that our desire for pleasure is too strong, but too weak! We have settled for a home, a family, a few friends, a job, a television, a microwave oven, an occasional night out, a yearly vacation, and per-

haps a personal computer. We have accustomed ourselves to such meager, short-lived pleasures that our capacity for joy has shriveled. And so our worship has shriveled.[4]

If we settle for that which is seen and temporal, we continually struggle to keep our worship and joy from shriveling up. What we need is a daily focusing of our vision on the glory of Christ, the object and quest of our joy. So whenever you fill out an application or send a résumé and get no response, don't get discouraged. Take the issue to the Lord in prayer and then meditate on the One who is the hope of glory, the joy of our salvation!

The Cure for a Downcast Spirit

How we respond when the troubles of life leave us feeling bruised and raw reveals where the object of our joy lies. This is the focus of Psalms 42 and 43, especially in the recurring refrain of 42:5–6, 42:11 and 43:5:

> Why are you cast down, O my soul,
>   and why are you in turmoil within me?
> Hope in God; for I shall again praise him,
>   my salvation and my God.

A downcast spirit refers to the feelings of discouragement and depression which arise because of life's circumstances. The psalmist identifies several causes of depression.

Depression arises from missing worship. The psalmist says his soul pants and thirsts for fellowship and communion with the Lord (42:1). He appears to be exiled in a distant land, far from the temple where he worshiped (42:2). His absence from corporate worship led to feelings of loneliness and depression.

We can experience the same feelings when we are separated from corporate worship. That is the catch-22: discouraging trials like joblessness shrivel our joy. As a result, we tend to be lethargic and apathetic toward corporate worship—the very thing we need most. Unless we break the cycle, it can spiral downward into despair.

Depression arises from hearing disparaging words. The taunt, "Where is your God?" (42:3, 10) can be intimidating. "If God loves you, why won't He answer your prayer?" can cut deep, as well as the spiritually crippling "If God is so good, where is He in your moment of need?" We may hear such words from unbelievers (42:3), but these discouraging thoughts are just as likely to arise in our own minds.

At times like this we want God to show up like He did for Shadrach, Meshach and Abednego (Dan. 3). We may think we want a clear display that God answers prayer, but what we really want is for God to answer *our* prayers according to *our* agenda. When He doesn't, the words of doubt and mocking can haunt us, only sinking us further into discouragement.

Depression arises from reflecting on better "days gone by." It is easy for us to think back to the past and long to relive those times (42:4); unfortunately, we often exaggerate the earlier times and see them as "glory days." The Israelites suffered oppressive slavery in Egypt, but when wandering in the desert, they foolishly longed for those "good old days" of abundant food: "We remember the fish we ate in Egypt that cost nothing, the cucumbers, the melons, the leeks, the onions, and the garlic" (Num. 11:5).

Dwelling on supposedly better "days gone by" leads, not surprisingly, to discontentment, as well as its inevitable byproducts, discouragement and depression. In unemployment our tendency is to look back on the previous job this way. Every job has its fair share of problems, but when times are tough, we are liable to forget the problems and exaggerate the good. This often drives us further down the path of depression.

Depression arises from focusing on the hardships of life. The waves and breakers, and the roar of the Lord's waterfalls (42:7) seem to be metaphors for the trials and hardships of life which have befallen the psalmist. Trials are part of life in a fallen world. If we insist on dwelling and lamenting our troubles, discouragement is soon to follow.

Our spiritual myopia makes our problems, and especially our unemployment situation, loom so large that we think we are worse off than anyone else. The more we dwell on our circumstances, the worse they appear. The worse they appear, the more downcast our spirits become. When I lost my job, I was consumed by the circumstances of my life. It was all I could focus on, and there were many days I didn't even want to get out of bed in the morning. I had allowed my joy to be stolen by the hardships of life.

Depression arises from our impatience when God does not seem to act. The longer we travel through difficulty, the more likely we are to ask, "Lord, why aren't You acting? Why do You delay?" We may even spiritualize the issue by saying, "Lord, if only You would act quickly, consider the witness and how it would bring glory to Your name!"

God almost never works in our time frame or in the way we expect. We can never anticipate His motives, plans and actions, because He declares that "as the heavens are higher than the earth, so are my ways higher than your ways and my thoughts than your thoughts" (Isa. 55:9). We may know this intellectually, but not emotionally, so frustration sets in, and we become exasperated at what appears to be God's unwillingness to act on our behalf. We may even begin to think God is somehow punishing us, which only makes us sink further into despondency.

Depression arises from being hurt by ungodly persons. When we suffer at the hands of the ungodly, it stings, but the pain is intensified when we see the ungodly succeed and advance in this world (43:1). This can cause us to wonder if the Lord has rejected us (43:2). Joblessness often generates feelings of abandonment; when we see others succeeding, it only knocks us down further.

Biblical hope is not wishful thinking; it is making God the ultimate object of our trust and confidence.

The cure for depression is hope in God. Where can we turn when our soul is downcast? What can we do when our spirits are swamped in despondency? The repeated refrain in these two psalms gives the cure for a downcast spirit: "Hope in God; for I shall again praise him, my salvation and my God." Biblical hope is not wishful thinking; it is making God the ultimate object of our trust and confidence.

What is the object of the psalmist's hope? It is not a circumstance; it is a person. His praise is in his God who never changes (Mal. 3:6). How do we maintain our focus on the hope of our salvation? The psalmist asks the Lord to "send out your light and your truth; let them lead me; let them bring me to your holy hill and to your dwelling!" (Ps. 43:3).

The only way to battle deceptive, discouraging thoughts is to rest upon the truth of God's Word. By the power of the Spirit working through the Scriptures, we can look past those distressing circumstances which lead to darkness and desolation.

Being without work can leave us feeling alone. The weight of joblessness and providing for our families can beat on us like relentless ocean waves. We must fix our bearings on Christ. To center our joy on any other object will only lead to discouragement and disillusionment. We might need to return again and again to this lesson. The pull toward finding joy in circumstances and the things which are seen is strong. We need to spend time every day in God's Word, soaking in the marvelous vision of the glory of God in the face of Christ—the treasure contained in jars of clay (2 Cor. 4:6–7).

Chapter Six

Growing in Perseverance

Wading through joblessness can seem like a never-ending nightmare, and it is a struggle just to keep going. The hardest part of the journey is the waiting. The days seem to tick away at a pace that at times may seem unbearably slow. My wife and I mentioned this to another couple at a church function who had asked how we were handling the difficulties of unemployment. Their response was both simple and profound: "God often answers prayer in the eleventh hour."

God's timing does not often align with ours. It seems as if He waits until things are just about lost before He answers. (Perhaps He does it that way to leave no doubt that the answer is from Him.) The difficulty with any kind of trial, and the cause of much of our anxiety, is that we do not know how long we must wait. We naturally try to get out from under a burden as soon as we can, but we lose so much by doing so. As Richard Hendrix points out, "Second only to suffering, waiting may be the greatest teacher and trainer in godliness, maturity, and genuine spirituality most of us ever encounter."[1] It is in waiting that we discover the jewel of sanctification—God's molding process by which we become holy as He is holy. This is God's will for us.

If we are honest with ourselves, we are impatient people. We live in a society of instant gratification, with no appreciation for the value of perseverance. Financial scams and get-rich-quick schemes hold out the promise of an alluring alternative to working long, hard hours for thirty or forty years. A plethora of diet pills tell us we can lose weight in a few weeks rather than the slow and difficult process of changing our eating and exercise habits. We are unwilling to endure pain or difficulty, so we have mastered the art of finding shortcuts.

But when we attempt to do this in our spiritual lives, we discover there are no "ten easy steps" to Christ-likeness, no shortcut to spiritual maturity. It is a life-long process. Moses lived as a shepherd in the wilderness of Midian for forty years before the Lord called him to lead his people out of Egypt. David was anointed king of Israel, but had to wait nearly two decades before taking the throne. Paul was called to be the apostle to the Gentiles (Acts 9:15) but apparently spent three years in preparation before he began his ministry (Gal. 1:15–18). The Lord uses extended times of waiting to shape and mold our character and to prepare us for His purposes.

Our impatience with God's perfect timing only makes the wait longer and the journey more exhausting. We need to see impatience as more than a character flaw or shortcoming; impatience is sin. It is a sign of unbelief—unbelief in God's power and ability, unbelief in the goodness of God's perfect will.

But I would not be honest if I did not admit that unemployment takes its toll on our emotional and spiritual state. Each wearisome day brings new levels of frustration. Each step becomes harder to take. If we are going to victoriously walk by faith through unemployment, we need to trust the Holy Spirit to "awaken and solidify rugged, Christ-exalting endurance" within us.[2]

Promises for Perseverance

The epistle of James was written to Christians who were suffering persecution, which appears to have resulted in economic hardship as well. You might even say that opposition to their faith led them to experience unemployment or underemployment and unfair wages. James does not ignore the injustice of the situation. Speaking to their rich oppressors, he declared, "The wages of the laborers who mowed your fields, which you kept back by fraud, are crying out against you" (5:4).

Be it due to religious persecution or tough economic times, the gulf between "the haves" and "the have-nots" often causes resentment against those who seem to profit off the backs of common laborers. Outrage and frustration is directed toward the ones who "have lived on the earth in luxury and in self-indulgence" (5:5). Does James call for the poor of the world to unite? Does he urge the oppressed to rise up and protest? Absolutely not; instead he calls us to be patient.

> Be patient; therefore, brothers, until the coming of the Lord. See how the farmer waits for the precious fruit of the earth, being patient about it, until it receives the early and the late rains. You also, be patient. Establish your

hearts, for the coming of the Lord is at hand. Do not grumble against one another, brothers, so that you may not be judged; behold, the Judge is standing at the door. As an example of suffering and patience, brothers, take the prophets who spoke in the name of the Lord. Behold we consider those blessed who remain steadfast. You have heard of the steadfastness of Job, and you have seen the purpose of the Lord, how the Lord is compassionate and merciful. (5:7–12)

When we are laid off, take a pay cut, get downsized or receive some other financial blow, we have to endure and persevere. We can trust that God is at work in us and will bring it to completion at the day of Jesus Christ. But until then, God often takes us down some difficult roads. Be patient. Remain steadfast. Establish your heart in the truth.

A diamond is created only under pressure; if it did not endure the pressure, it would just be a lump of coal.

Patience is the ability to remain under the pressures of life, knowing it is God's best for us. A diamond is created only under pressure; if it did not endure the pressure, it would just be a lump of coal. It is when we remain steadfast that we become spiritually complete, lacking in nothing (James 1:4). How can we remain patient when we are overloaded with troubles? James provides three promises that we can hang onto.

Promise 1: The Lord Is Returning

The second coming of Christ is mentioned twice in this

passage (vv. 7–8). Nothing provides hope like the promise of the coming of the Lord. If we remind ourselves that the return of Christ could happen at any moment, we can persevere in our afflictions, knowing that they are temporary and "not worthy to be compared with the glory that is to be revealed to us" (Rom. 8:18).

Since Christ could return in the twinkling of an eye (1 Cor. 15:52), we ought to live with that expectancy. The promise of His coming does not remove the immediacy of the trial or lessen its discomfort, but it does put it in proper perspective. We are sojourners and pilgrims (1 Pet. 2:11); this world is not our home; our citizenship is in heaven (Phil. 3:20). So whether we find ourselves in economic hardship or something worse, knowing that His return is near gives us the hope to endure and the patience to remain steadfast.

Promise 2: The Lord Is Returning in Judgment

Christ will return to judge the world, with all the authority the Father has given Him (John 5:22). His judgments are and will be perfect and just. "He shall not judge by what his eyes see, or decide disputes by what his ears hear, but with righteousness he shall judge the poor, and decide with equity for the meek of the earth" (Isa. 11:3–4). This too gives us hope to endure.

Many of the hardships we have to endure seem unfair—and they often are. There is a lot of injustice in our world, and at times we fall victim to it. And yet, even when job loss is not the result of an obvious and blatant injustice, it is easy to feel like a victim. If we take on the victim role, we start looking for someone to blame, and we begin to grumble against others. If we are not careful, this victim mentality can develop into a deep-seated bitterness. What can keep us from growing impatient with our circumstances and people we feel might be responsible or associated with the issue? It is trusting in the Lord and His justice (Rom. 12:19).

When Christ returns, "each one's work will become manifest, for the Day will disclose it, because it will be revealed by fire, and the fire will test what sort of work each one has done. If the work that anyone has built on the foundation survives, he will receive a reward" (1 Cor. 3:13–14). We all will stand before the judgment seat of Christ. Therefore, this also should encourage us to be patient with others and to endure suffering. The Lord will hold us accountable for how we respond to our lot in life.

Promise 3: The Lord Will Bless Those Who Remain Steadfast

James 5:11 promises that those who endure will be blessed. Though we may not be able to see how it is possible to be blessed when struggling through joblessness, we must trust in the depth of God's compassion and mercy. It is the mercy, steadfast love and faithfulness of the Lord which preserves us through trials (Ps. 40:11).

The foremost means by which the Lord shows His mercy and compassion to us is in our salvation, but He does so in many other ways as well, such as His comfort in our hardships and trials. Paul tells us that His comfort is so overflowing that we are able to comfort others (2 Cor. 1:4).

This is the testimony of Joseph, who was sold into slavery by his brothers, then falsely accused of attempted rape and thrown in jail. But through the love, mercy and faithfulness of the Lord, he remained steadfast and persevered, even when his situation seemed hopeless. In the end he saw the Lord's hand turn his hardships into blessings—blessings which overflowed to many others, including his brothers, the very ones who had mistreated him! "As for you, you meant evil against me, but God meant it for good, to bring it about that many people should be kept alive, as they are today" (Gen. 50:20).

Examples of Perseverance

Patience can start to seem very abstract when the weeks pass by with no news on the job front; it drains us of energy and the will to keep going. What we need is to see perseverance in action—examples we can follow. James gives us three such examples, each with its own unique perspective.

Just as the farmer trusts in the providential working of God to produce the harvest, we must depend upon the sovereignty of God as we go through the dry and difficult seasons.

1. The Farmer: Persevering through the Seasons of Life

The goal of the farmer is the harvest—a bountiful supply to sustain him and his family for the coming year. If the harvest does not come, it is economically devastating for the family. So the farmer keeps his eye on the goal and works toward it. But there's no rushing the harvest. The farmer must patiently do his part and then wait for the life-giving rains which bring the increase.

The text refers to the early and late rains. In the Palestinian region the early rains follow the planting stage. The farmer plows and tills the land and plants the seed; he may even fertilize the soil. But for the seed to germinate and take root, it takes rain. Rain is out of the farmer's control; he must wait and be patient.

The late rains, which come after the seed sprouts and begins to bear fruit, provide the moisture needed to bring the crop to full maturity for the harvest. Prolonged periods of extreme dryness often occur between the early and late rains. If the farmer allows the dry periods to discourage him, he may give up on the crop, miss the harvest and lose everything. The farmer must patiently wait through each season.

As we go through the various seasons in life, we too must wait upon the Lord and be patient. Just as the farmer trusts in the providential working of God to produce the harvest, we must depend upon the sovereignty of God as we go through the dry and difficult seasons. God is the One who controls the rains which the farmer relies upon for the harvest. God is also the One who controls the circumstances of our life so that we bear much fruit. This will include seasons of pruning. But when we persevere and continue in the faith, in due season our lives will produce patience—as well as all the other aspects of the fruit of the Spirit (Gal. 5:22).

2. The Prophets: Persevering through the Suffering of Life

From the patient waiting of the farmer, James turns to the example of the patient endurance of the prophets who, because of their commitment and devotion to the Lord,

> . . . suffered mocking and flogging, and even chains and imprisonment. They were stoned, they were sawn in two, they were killed with the sword. They went about in skins of sheep and goats, destitute, afflicted, mistreated—of

whom the world was not worthy—wandering about
in deserts and mountains, and in dens and caves of the
earth. (Heb. 11:36–38)

When Ezekiel was called to be a prophet, God told him
that his message would not be received well: "Be not afraid
of them, nor be afraid of their words, though briers and
thorns are with you and you sit on scorpions. Be not afraid
of their words, nor be dismayed at their looks, for they are a
rebellious house" (Ezekiel 2:6). For nearly twenty years Ezekiel was ridiculed, opposed and faced hardship because of
the message he proclaimed. Nevertheless, he persevered.

Daniel is another example of suffering with patience.
Several times he faced the prospect of losing his life because
of his commitment to the Lord. One such occasion was
when he was thrown into the lions' den. With such insurmountable odds against him, Daniel entrusted his life to the
sovereign Lord and remained steadfast.

Jeremiah, the epitome of suffering, served the Lord as
a prophet for over forty years, facing repeated antagonism
and persecution from the religious and political authori-
ties. The leaders of his hometown of Anathoth conspired
to kill him because they hated the message he proclaimed
(Jer. 11:18–23). The priest Pashhur, outraged against Jeremiah's preaching, beat him and had him put in chains (Jer.
20:1–6). Jeremiah was even falsely accused of treason (Jer.
37:11–15). Yet during the more than four decades he "spoke
in the name of the Lord," he was a pillar of perseverance in
the midst of suffering.

When suffering in life comes, the call is to remain patient. We must wait upon the Lord and trust in His unwavering faithfulness. God might not take us up to heaven in a

whirlwind (2 Kings 2:1) or save us from a lions' den (Dan. 6:22–23), but His grace is still sufficient, and His power is made perfect in our weakness (2 Cor. 12:7). He calls some to persevere to the point of martyrdom, and others are to remain faithful through the pain of a trial like unemployment. Regardless, the call remains the same: "Be patient, brothers, until the coming of the Lord" (James 5:7).

3. Job: Persevering through the Silence of Life

James' final example is Job. Who can relate to the level of suffering Job was asked to endure? We may suffer the death of a loved one or the loss of our health, our income or our possessions, but to lose all these at once—in a single day? It is a burden reserved for only a rare handful.

And yet, Job is known not only for his great suffering, but for a different type of hardship he faced: a hardship of *silence*. This is something we can surely relate to. Sometimes when trouble comes, heaven seems silent. We don't know why our problems began or when they will end. The more we cry out to God, the less He seems to respond. The silence is deafening.

Job's servants were murdered by marauders, his fields consumed by fire, and his children killed in a natural disaster (Job 1:13–19); he was afflicted with "loathsome sores from the sole of his foot to the crown of his head" (2:7). Job could not understand why all this happened to him. Yet through it all he was able to say, "Naked I came from my mother's womb, and naked shall I return. The LORD gave, and the LORD has taken away; blessed be the name of the LORD" (1:21). In all his suffering Job did not sin or charge God with wrong (1:22; 2:10). Though unable to peer behind the curtain at the scene playing out in the heavens (1:6–12), Job persevered, even when all heaven seemed silent. When God finally did speak, Job was the one left silent, with nothing to say (Job 40:3–5).

Many of us will never fully understand, in this life, the reason for some of our times of pain, loneliness and hardship, and the silence can be almost unbearable. But notice that when God finally broke His silence and spoke to Job, He still did not explain His actions. God brought Job beyond the need for an explanation to the point of trust. Job is a powerful illustration of patience and perseverance through the silence of life's struggles.

Regardless of our situation, the key to perseverance when things don't make sense is to refocus our vision on the majestic character of God. When the Lord questioned Job, he was overwhelmed with the extent of God's greatness, majesty and sovereignty. This vision of who God is did not change the circumstances, but it did change his perspective: "I know that you can do all things, and that no purpose of yours can be thwarted. . . . Therefore I have uttered what I did not understand, things too wonderful for me, which I did not know" (Job 42:2–3). When Job remained steadfast, he received the blessing of seeing the Lord in His glory.

The ability to persevere through times of unemployment comes from an enlarged vision of God's greatness. When we struggle with the doubts and fears of being out of work, it is because we have a faulty view of God, doubting His sovereignty, ability or love. But when we have a right perspective of the greatness of God, through His grace we can face seemingly insurmountable obstacles and remain steadfast in our faith.

Disciplines for Growing in Perseverance

To be a successful athlete takes perseverance and patience. Trophies are not won overnight; they take time and diligent effort. This picture of patient endurance through years of intense training is what Paul had in mind when he wrote, "Train yourself for godliness; for while bodily training is of some value, godliness is of value in every way, as it holds promise for the present life and also for the life to come" (1 Tim. 4:7–8).

A high school classmate of mine won numerous trophies for weightlifting. I was also a weightlifter, but without the success he enjoyed. Was it genetics or natural ability? Maybe, but the real difference between us was his patient endurance. While he consistently endured long hours of training, I became sidetracked and moved on to other things. This is why he flourished, and my training never produced significant results.

The two most important exercises for spiritual fitness are Bible study and prayer. Consistent time in the Word of God, which includes both meditation and memorization, is indispensable.

Spiritually, we need to train ourselves with the intensity of a winning athlete. (It is no coincidence that the word translated "training" in First Timothy 4:7 is related to the word "gymnasium.") Growth in the Christ-centered life requires the same kind of discipline, exercise and practice as the athlete sweating it out in the gym. Physical training involves *diet, exercise* and *persistence*. The same three elements are associated with training in godliness.

The proper *diet* for spiritual training is the Word of God. Like Jeremiah, we must feed on the Word of God and let it become a joy and delight to our hearts (Jer. 15:16). Without a daily intake of Scripture, we starve ourselves and become spiritually famished: "Man shall not live by bread alone, but by every word that comes from the mouth of God" (Matt. 4:4). It is regular meditation and study of God's Word which gives us the strength to endure.

Training in godliness also entails rigorous *exercise*. The two most important exercises for spiritual fitness are Bible study and prayer. Consistent time in the Word of God, which includes both meditation and memorization, is indispensable. When facing the trials of life, focus on those passages which build up confidence and trust, and provide hope and encouragement.

Biblical meditation is not an emptying of the mind (as is taught in Eastern mysticism), but a filling of the mind with the words of Scripture. It is delving into and mulling over the text, understanding the central idea and considering how it can be applied in daily living. After meditating on the Word, pray through the passage, asking God to fulfill its truths and promises in your own life. Meditation is taking the time not only to be in the Word but to allow the Word to get into you.

Memorization of Scripture also has numerous benefits. It is a storehouse of truth for all occasions. It offers words of comfort in times of suffering. It brings to mind strengthening promises in times of weakness. It provides wisdom for daily decisions.

Memorization also assists in the process of sanctification. Unemployment often brings to the surface sinful attitudes and habits; as they surface, the Spirit brings to our minds memorized verses, which lead us to godly grief and true repentance (2 Cor. 7:9–10). This is what spiritual growth and sanctification is all about.

To store God's Word in one's heart and mind is what the apostle Paul meant when he instructed believers to let the "word of Christ dwell in you richly" (Col. 3:16). To have Scripture dwell in us is to have it become so ingrained that it directs our lives. This is critical if we are going to allow an extended time of joblessness transform us more into the likeness of Christ.

Prayer is also a means of exercising our faith in response to the rigors of life's challenges. God welcomes and invites us to commune with Him in prayer and to share with Him our needs: "And this is the confidence that we have toward Him, that if we ask anything according to His will he hears us. And if we know that He hears us in whatever we ask, we know that we have the requests that we have asked of Him" (1 John 5:14– 15). This passage does not mean we always get everything we ask of God. Sometimes God does provide specifically what we pray for. But at other times, we pray for what we think we need or what seems best, the Lord answers by providing something even better.

When the nation of Israel prayed to God to deliver them from the bondage of Egypt, the Lord God remembered the covenant He made with them and promised them far more than me re deliverance from bondage:

> I will redeem you with an outstretched arm and with
> great acts of judgment. I will take you to be my people,

and I will be your God, and you shall know that I am the Lord your God, who has brought you out from under the burdens of the Egyptians. I will bring you into the land that I swore to give to Abraham, Isaac and to Jacob. I will give it to you for a possession. I am the LORD. (Exod. 6:6–9)

Yet there are times when we earnestly pray for God to move or act in a particular way and it appears as if we do not receive any answer. This does not mean that God did not hear. It also does not mean God did not answer. We can be sure that, in the infinite wisdom of God, He is doing something even greater than what we asked for, though it means that for a season we feel exhausted, bankrupt and destitute.

We have already looked at the example set for us in the suffering of the prophets, especially Jeremiah. He is also our example in the intensity and earnestness of his prayers. The book of Lamentations expresses Jeremiah's grief, but also shows his prayerful hope in God and his reliance on God's grace and mercy as he continually cried out in mourning for the nation.

Jeremiah did not live to see the fulfillment of his hope of a restored Israel. Does this mean God did not answer? Does it mean that He did not hear Jeremiah's prayers? Not at all! God had a bigger plan in place which reached much further than just the restoration of Israel to include the ransom of people for God "from every tribe and language and people and nation" (Rev. 5:9).

We see the true power of prayer as the Holy Spirit uses our prayers to change our perspective more than our circumstances. During my journey of joblessness, I repeatedly prayed for the Lord to open up a position. After a number of interviews in which my hopes were raised, only to eventually have the door closed, my prayers began to change. As new positions come my way, I still take them before the Lord, but with the mindset of "Lord, not my will, but Yours."

My own prayers changed when I came to the point of surrendering my dreams and desires, laying them at the foot of the cross. My prayers are now less focused on a particular job opportunity and more on the desire for God to be glorified in me. The Holy Spirit is transforming me into the likeness of Christ—but only as I persist in my prayer life.

If we are going to experience growth in the Christ-centered life, we need to persist and remain steadfast under the pressure of life's hardships.

This is why *persistence* is the underlying element for success in training. Without it we eventually give up on diet and exercise. To be honest, I never really liked the slogan "no pain, no gain"—which is probably why I never excelled in sports—but it has a great deal of truth in it. Most of us want to avoid pain, and it is true that some pain is harmful, but a certain amount of pain is the path to growth. If we are going to experience growth in the Christ-centered life, we need to persist and remain steadfast under the pressure of life's hardships.

When I did weightlifting, one thing that helped me persist was working out with others. They became a support group to spur me on and encourage me to not give up. They also motivated me to keep on by their diligent example. The same is true in our Christian walk. Our willingness to persist is bolstered by the example of godly men and women whose endurance of past and present trials exalts and glorifies Christ.

Paul encouraged the church to imitate him and to walk according to the example he provided (Phil. 3:17). He is a great example to imitate because he endured so many hardships throughout his life (2 Cor. 11:23–27). Look for examples of individuals who have weathered trials in a God-honoring and Christ-exalting manner.

In addition to the numerous examples in Scripture, there are many from church history—John Bunyan, John Calvin, Martin Luther, William Carey and David Brainerd to name a few. Also consider examples of faithful believers you know personally. Who are the men and women in your life who exemplify that spirit of pressing on with steadfast faith in the midst of adversity, hardship and tribulation? Take note of how they rested in their identity in Christ. Observe how they humbly depended upon the Lord, trusting in His sovereignty and goodness. Pay attention to the contentment they exhibited in the harsh conditions of life. Witness the Object of their joy and gladness. Therefore, "since we are surrounded by so great a cloud of witnesses [of those who remained faithful], let us run with endurance the race that is set before us" (Heb. 12:1).

Perseverance is not an easy lesson to learn. There will be times when we are weary, but we must continue to walk by faith and not by sight (2 Cor. 5:7), remaining under the Father's pruning so that we bear fruit in our spiritual lives (John 15:2). If we endure through the pain of training in the "spiritual gymnasium" of life, we will grow strong in our faith and in the likeness of Christ.

Section Three

The Jewel of Thanksgiving

*Give thanks in all circumstances; for this is the will of God
in Christ Jesus for you.* (1 Thess. 5:18)

A re we really to give thanks in *all* circumstances? Surely
the Lord must be willing to grant some exceptions.
Maybe this is a bad translation. Could it be that the word
"all" isn't even in the original text? It seems like a lot to ask
of someone who is hurting and troubled to not only endure
and persevere, but *also* to give thanks!

These were some of the thoughts that ran through my
mind when I read this verse during one of my quiet times
with the Lord. Yet it is not a suggestion, not an option, not
simply a "nice idea" we are free to ignore. Giving thanks in
all circumstances is a *command*.

We often waste too much time on the details, challenges
and "what ifs" of our situation. If we let the circumstances of
life become the focal point of our thinking, unemployment
can become all-encompassing in our minds. When this happens, it affects how we view ourselves (our identity) and can
cause a crisis of belief that can lead to pride, discontent, lack

of joy and weariness. This is carnal thinking, living by the flesh and not by the Spirit.

Genuine thanksgiving moves beyond circumstances. Thanksgiving to God is a command, but it is also a choice we have to make. Just as Joshua called the Israelites to choose whom they would serve (Josh. 24:15), we must choose where our focus will be—on Christ or our circumstances. The choice is between setting one's mind on things above or things on the earth (Col. 3:2).

If we have truly been born again, giving thanks in all circumstances is not a choice we can ignore. Being thankful is part of God's will for our lives. To give thanks in the midst of our trials ascribes glory to God and proclaims in the midst of a sin-cursed world that the Lord is worthy of praise. The heart of giving thanks in all circumstances is setting one's mind upon the eternal riches of the gospel message. Having a gospel-informed and gospel-driven perspective which rests solely upon the grace and sovereignty of God enables us to give thanks for the testing of our faith and the treasure of our faith.

Chapter Seven

Giving Thanks for the Testing of Our Faith

Do you know *anyone* who actually *enjoys* hardship and adversity? Of course not! We all dread trials, and one reason is that all trials involve a sense of loss.

From unemployment to illness to the death of a loved one, loss is at the center. In joblessness it is the loss of work, income and financial security. In illness it is loss of health. In death it is the loss of relationship. That's one reason trials are so painful—the loss changes our circumstances and brings us into unknown territory. Humility, contentment, joy and perseverance become a struggle because we just do not know how things will turn out.

When I was out of work, I hit some deep emotional low points; at times I cried out, "Jesus, how much more? Where is the end of the road?" I found it very hard during these times even to think about giving thanks. So how do we live out First Thessalonians 5:18—"Give thanks in all circumstances . . ."?

Giving Thanks and Faith

There is a clear connection between faith and thankfulness. If we do not have a right view of God—if we do not trust in His goodness, power, wisdom and justice—then pride, discontentment, discouragement and despair rise to the surface, and we cry "Foul!" Instead of being thankful for what God has given us, we are tempted to protest the violation of our rights and demand justice. This can lead us to doubt and question our faith.

True faith involves the whole person—
mind, heart and will.

How does the Bible define faith? As used in the Scriptures, the word implies both trust and allegiance. The Old and New Testaments use a variety of words to express this meaning, but they all point to the firmness and reliability of the object being trusted, as well as the idea of leaning one's full weight upon the object of faith. True faith involves the whole person—mind, heart and will.

For example, you may be sitting in a chair right now. Before you sat down, did you need to be persuaded in your thinking that the chair was able to hold your weight? Probably not; you did not give it much thought at all. You just sat down, and in that simple act you demonstrated that your mind and heart trusted in the reliability of the chair. That is faith.

Biblical faith is trust in the Person of Christ Himself. He is the one to whom we give our allegiance, trusting in his sacrificial atonement and victory over death and sin. It is being persuaded in our minds that what Scripture teaches is true and accurate, and trusting in the reliability of God's promises. Since genuine faith is always seen in action, in obedience—in what we do, not just what we say—the out-working of such faith is a surrender of one's life and will to Christ.

But while saving faith has a definite beginning point—conversion—it does not stop there; it continues to grow throughout our remaining days here on earth. Faith is not only critical in justification but also in the progressive work of sanctification—and it is here that we see a clear connection between faith and thankfulness..

Grumbling about our circumstances shows a lack of faith. Why? Because it questions the sovereignty and goodness of the One who directs our steps (Jer. 10:23). Our complaints reveal a discontentment with God's gracious provision for us. When we sink into discouragement and lose our joy over the circumstances of life, it is obvious that the object of our joy is something other than Christ alone. When we doubt God's wisdom, authority, ability and goodness, we are unable to give thanks sincerely.

That is why the first step to giving thanks is to rest in the sovereignty of God. Just as saving faith "depends not on human will or exertion, but on God, who has mercy" (Rom. 9:16), the work of sanctification continues to rest in the sovereignty of God, "knowing that he who began a good work in you will bring it to completion at the day of Jesus Christ" (Phil. 1:6).

Resting in the sovereignty of God means acknowledging that He owns everything and owes us nothing. Everything is a gift from God (James 1:17), including our job, our possessions, our health—even our faith! Once we understand that even faith is one of God's gracious gifts, we can be thankful for the testing of our faith.

The Value of a Tested Faith

Faith in Christ does not make us immune to trials; they are an inevitable reality of life. And Peter makes the surprising declaration that they are actually good for us!

> Though for a little while, if necessary, you have been grieved by various trials, so that the tested genuineness of your faith—more precious than gold that perishes though it is tested by fire—may be found to result in praise and glory and honor at the revelation of Jesus Christ. (1 Pet. 1:6–7)

If we can view our "various trials" as the furnace which proves and refines the genuineness of our faith, it will help us to give thanks in the midst of hardship. How we respond to trials determines if they are more of a temptation against our faith or a proving ground for our faith.[1]

No matter how lonely the road we travel or painful the affliction we suffer, our trials are only "for a little while."

First Peter 1 reminds us what we are to give thanks for in tough times. When we are out of work, and tempted to forget the rich blessings we have received from the Lord, we need to focus our minds on our hope, the preciousness of our faith and the outcome of our faith.

Tested Faith Is Grounded in Living Hope

True faith is grounded in a living hope in the resurrection of Christ, which assures us of eternal life and an imperishable inheritance reserved for us in heaven (1 Pet. 1:3–4). If our salvation is secure and kept for us in heaven, then no form of tribulation, distress or persecution can separate us from the love of Christ (Rom. 8:35). This is our glorious hope!

No matter how lonely the road we travel or painful the affliction we suffer, our trials are only "for a little while" (1 Pet. 1:7). Even if they persist for a lifetime, compared to eternity they are of little consequence (Rom. 8:18). And when the former things have passed away and the Father restores all creation, there will be no more pain or suffering or trials (Rev. 21:3–4). Knowing all this, is there any reason not to give thanks to God?

Tested Faith Is More Precious than Riches

Since biblical faith is grounded on the living hope of the salvation of our souls, it is more precious than any earthly treasure; nothing this world offers can compare to the riches we have in Christ Jesus. This is another reason why we can give thanks. But Peter goes one step further by using the refining process of gold to illustrate the pricelessness of a tested faith.

Throughout history gold has been considered the most precious commodity in the world. Though today there some metals of greater value, gold is still the ultimate symbol of wealth and prosperity and the purer the gold, the more valuable it is.

Goldsmiths use the process of smelting to burn away impurities. The ore is placed in a crucible and subjected to the intense heat of the furnace. The metal turns to liquid form; the impurities—known as dross—rise to the surface and are skimmed off. The more the gold goes through this process, and the greater the intensity of the refining fire, the more impurities are burned away. What is left is genuine gold.

A similar process occurs when God puts His people through various trials: "For he is like a refiner's fire and like fullers' soap. He will sit as a refiner and purifier of silver, and he will purify the sons of Levi and refine them like gold and silver, and they will bring offerings in righteousness to the Lord" (Mal. 3:2–3).

Fullers' soap is a lye soap used to clean garments and make them white as snow. Like the refiner's fire, it refers to the cleansing and purifying process the Lord takes His people through. Solomon makes a similar point when he writes, "the crucible is for silver, and the furnace is for gold, and the Lord tests hearts" (Prov. 17:3). We should desire 24-karat faith.

Trials are the refining process of our faith. The Lord refines us in the fire of suffering and hardship to make us pure and holy. "For you, O God, have tested us; you have tried us as silver is tried" (Ps. 66:10). God's people are to praise Him for this testing because through it He brings us to the place of abundance (66:12)—to a deeper fellowship and union with Him and to greater passion for worship and service rendered to Him (66:13–15).

So how can we give thanks in our circumstances? We can when we understand that affliction, though difficult and painful, is the way God purifies our faith—burning away the unbelief, impurity and filth which remain in our lives. Is the intensity of the refiner's fire enjoyable? Hardly! Is being rubbed raw by caustic fullers' soap something delightful? Not on your life! But is the intense heat of the furnace of affliction profitable? Absolutely! The Lord is molding us to be more like Christ and proving the "tested genuineness" of our faith.

We can rejoice in the midst of trials, knowing that
God is at work purifying our souls.

The idea of "tested genuineness" comes from the field of metalworking. Testing refers to the process of appraising ore to determine the quality of the precious metal it contains. The testing process evaluates "a metal's purity and determines its true content and worth after all impurities have been smelted away."[2]

Not only can we rejoice in the midst of trials, knowing that God is at work purifying our souls, but we rejoice in the goal of the refining process: "praise and glory and honor at the revelation of Jesus Christ" (1 Pet. 1:7). Whether this praise is being directed to the people of God or to Christ, we know that the praise will still be given back to the Lord. Whatever praise, rewards or crowns we may receive in heaven will be cast down at the feet of Jesus, and we will say, "To him who sits on the throne and to the Lamb, be blessing and honor and glory and might forever and ever!" (Rev. 5:13).

Tested Faith Results in Spiritual Maturity

A passage with many similarities to First Peter 1:6–7 is James 1:2–4: "Count it all joy, my brothers, when you meet trials of various kinds, for you know that the testing of your faith produces steadfastness. And let steadfastness have its full effect, that you may be perfect and complete, lacking nothing." Both passages direct the reader to see the value of giving thanks for the testing of our faith, and stress some of the specific benefits gained from trials.

The word "steadfastness" presents a picture of patient endurance and commitment, even when others give in to the pressure. True saving faith will persevere regardless of the intensity of the furnace's heat. Steadfastness is not the end goal, however, but only a step in the process of what God is ultimately doing in the lives of His people. The aim and purpose of trials is maturity—to become "perfect and complete."

To be "perfect" means to be fully developed or mature. It refers to something which has reached its intended goal or end. "Complete" refers to being whole, not lacking in any area. This means that the intended result of endurance in trials is sanctification. It is growth in spiritual maturity—developing a greater trust, reliance and dependence upon the sovereignty, goodness, faithfulness, grace and mercy of the Lord Jesus Christ. That is why we should not view trials like unemployment as harmful or destructive. As Warren Wiersbe puts it, they are a means of "weaning us away from childish things."[3] The key is how we react to the testing of our faith.

If we willingly surrender to the will of God while in the furnace of affliction and trust in His sovereignty and the sufficiency of His grace, we will come out on the other side stronger in faith and more committed to Christ. If out of pride, impatience and dissatisfaction we grumble, complain and become bitter, it reveals that we are either still immature in our faith or we never really belonged to Christ in the first place (1 John 2:19). We can give thanks for the testing of our faith, knowing it is God's design to bring us to the point of spiritual maturity.

Giving Thanks for the Testing of Our Faith

The paradox is this: unemployment can be a blessing. Don't misunderstand me; it is not an enjoyable place to be. The reason being out of work can be viewed as a blessing is the depth in which we can grow spiritually. My faith has much deeper roots of trust in the sovereignty of God than before this trial. My faith is stronger and better able to withstand the crashing waves of life's ordeals than when times were just humming along without incident.

My faith is far from perfect and complete. It is nowhere near 24-karat faith. But my faith is more pure than it was before this journey began. I still go through periods of time when my gaze drifts away from its glorious and radiant center, Jesus Christ. It remains a daily battle against anxiety, worry and stress, and I have to work at keeping my joy from being shriveled up over such things as food, shelter and clothing.

But I thank my God for the refiner's fire. Through joblessness He breaks down our self-reliance and our dependence upon personal resources and abilities. As the Potter, He molds our hearts to entrust everything—finances, family and future—into His loving care and provision. While we continue our efforts to find employment, we are blessed to

know we are not alone; we walk by faith with Jesus in the
job search.

Can your unemployment bring glory to God? It can,
if you approach it with a Christ-centered perspective.

This is how we turn joblessness into the backdrop to
shine like lights in our world. It is in the darkest days of
angst, doubts and fear that the glorious light of the knowledge of God's goodness shines brightest. He is the Giver of
all good gifts and we are to give Him, the Giver, all the glory
and praise and honor He deserves. And even at the lowest
point in our lives, our praise still resounds—not because of
gifts like our families, jobs or possessions, but simply because of the gift of God Himself.

Can your unemployment bring glory to God? Can joblessness become the refining fire to produce spiritual maturity and make your faith more pure and precious? It can,
if you approach it with a Christ-centered perspective. You
need to ask yourself: Am I going to depend on God or on
myself? Will I trust God's Word or my own plans? Let the
Refiner do His work in you, bringing to the surface the dross
of a self-dependent, self-promoting and self-pitying spirit.
Let Him burn away the impurities of discontent, doubt and
fear. Then you will be in the position to give thanks for the
testing of your faith.

Chapter Eight

Giving Thanks for the Treasure of Faith

H. Beecher Hicks, Jr. observes that everyone is either "coming out of a storm, in a storm, or heading for a storm."[1] Joblessness is like a major storm. When it strikes, it creates hurricane-force winds of doubt, torrential downpours of anxiety, flash floods of fear and worry. Will we persevere? Will our faith stand firm? It all depends on our foundation, and where our treasure lies.

At one particular point in my journey of living without work, I found myself spiraling downward, emotionally and spiritually. A couple of job opportunities had folded. Financial challenges started to mount. As I thought about the uncertain future, I sensed the anxiety rising. I seemed to be unraveling under the pressure of financial concerns, and I felt alone and helpless. I knew that something had to change, but as I looked ahead to the unknown, my doubts, anxiety and fear only intensified.

If we are to shine as lights along the journey of unemployment, we must address the areas of unbelief which hold us back. Our doubts stem from a lack of faith and trust in the sovereignty, power and goodness of God. Our questioning stems from a hesitation to believe God is in control of the situation and is willing to help us in our time of need. Our questioning also reveals what we treasure most and are afraid of losing.

We can't avoid hardship, but we can choose what direction it will take us.

"No one ever said they learned their deepest lessons of life, or had their sweetest encounters with God, on the sunny days," declares John Piper. "People go deep with God when the drought comes. That is the way God designed it. Christ aims to be magnified in life most clearly by the way we experience him in our losses."[2] We can't avoid hardship, but we can choose what direction it will take us. Every trial we encounter will either move us toward greater spiritual growth or spiral us downward into despair. No matter how difficult our trial may be, we can thank God for seasons of darkness because they highlight the magnificence and radiance of the treasure of our faith. When the dark clouds move in, we have an opportunity to shine the brightest by the way we magnify the treasure of knowing Christ.

The Treasures of Truth in Romans 8

Romans 8 is a passage of Scripture filled with hope and encouragement. It is a passage worth meditating on when going through hard times. Six gold nuggets of truth in Romans 8 point to our ultimate treasure and jewel. When we cling to and trust these promises, even if everything in life is stripped away, Christ Jesus will be glorified and magnified in and through our lives.

Treasure 1: Unmerited Pardon

The hope of the Christian faith is grounded in the promise that there is "no condemnation for those who are in Christ" (Rom. 8:1). This verse is pivotal to Paul's teaching throughout Romans on the doctrine of justification by faith alone, in which the repentant sinner is declared not guilty before God. Romans 8:1 comes right after Paul describes our battle with the flesh, which seduces us to do what we don't want to do and not do what we want to do (7:7–20). This battle with the sin nature leaves us crying out, "Wretched man that I am! Who will deliver me from this body of death?" (7:24).

If you were to stop reading at this verse, you would miss the treasure of your hope and wallow in the discouragement of your continual struggle with sin. Are you again under condemnation? Not at all! The very next verse assures us that we are set free from the law of sin and death, and Paul's argument then culminates in Romans 8:1, with its promise of "no condemnation."

A trial such as unemployment will bring to the surface deeply ingrained sin patterns in our lives, such as self-reliance, pride, anxiety, impatience and dissatisfaction. It is in the dark moments of doubt, when our faith is weak, that we find comfort in the promise that there is no condemnation. No matter how severe the adversity, no matter how much we still struggle between doing what we don't want to do and neglecting what we want to do, we can give thanks to God, through Jesus Christ our Lord, because we have been set free from the law of sin and death. This is a treasure that will never fade or spoil.

Treasure 2: The Indwelling Spirit

We are also blessed with the treasure of the Spirit of God dwelling in us: "If the Spirit of him who raised Jesus from the dead dwells in you, he who raised Christ Jesus from the dead will also give life to your mortal bodies through his Spirit who dwells in you" (Rom. 8:11). The emphasis of Romans 8:9–11 is our new life in Christ. Twice it mentions that the Spirit dwells in the children of God. What does this mean? John Stott explains: "The Christian life is essentially life in the Spirit, that is to say, a life which is animated, sustained, directed and enriched by the Holy Spirit. In other words, we are not on our own."[3]

Jesus said the same thing in John's Gospel when He promised to send the Spirit "to be with you forever, even the Spirit of truth, whom the world cannot receive, because it neither sees him nor knows him. You know him, for he dwells with you and will be in you" (14:16–17). The Spirit's work is as a Helper and Counselor to guide believers into truth (16:13).

His presence does not keep us from experiencing trials but strengthens us to endure and persevere through them.

There have been many times when I felt like I was all alone and no one understood what I was going through.

Much of the advice I heard ranged from empty platitudes, like "It's all right; everything will work out," to more stinging remarks, such as "If you really wanted a job you could have found one by now." Comments like this only made me feel that much more alone and isolated, and seemed to drain the life from me. It was such a comfort to know that the indwelling Holy Spirit understood my situation and would counsel me, help me and guide me in the truth.

The Spirit dwelling in us sustains, directs and enriches us, enabling us to experience the abundant life in Christ. The Father has given us His Spirit as an ever-present help, so we are never alone in out trials. His presence does not keep us from experiencing trials but strengthens us to endure and persevere through them. What a blessing and treasure it is to have the Spirit of the living God dwell in us.

Treasure 3: A Matchless Inheritance

Though we may suffer the loss of all we have in this world, we have been blessed with an eternal inheritance. John MacArthur notes that "The value of an inheritance is determined by the worth of the one who bequeaths it."[4] If that is true, we can then be assured of the infinite value of our eternal inheritance, which has been lavished on us by the Lord God Almighty, who owns everything: "The earth is the Lord's and the fullness thereof, the world and those who dwell therein" (Ps. 24:1).

One of the major stresses of unemployment is the potential of financial jeopardy. The loss of income can affect our ability to meet our basic financial needs. But Jesus told us not to worry about these things, because our heavenly Father knows we need them (Matt. 6:31–32). Focusing on the future inheritance that is reserved for us in heaven enables us to trust God for our provision today. "He who did not spare his own Son but gave him up for us all, how will he not also with him graciously give us all things?" (Rom. 8:32).

If we face the prospect of financial loss, can we honestly say, "The Lord gave, and the Lord has taken away; blessed be the name of the Lord" (Job 1:21)? Living well in the midst of joblessness and economic uncertainty is to set our joy upon the treasure of our matchless inheritance as the children of God. No economic downturn can take away or reduce this blessed inheritance. No trial can tarnish or deteriorate what the Father has given (Matt. 6:19-20). The hardship of unemployment has only made the words of an old gospel song more real to me:

> I'd rather have Jesus than silver or gold;
> I'd rather be His than have riches untold.
> I'd rather have Jesus than houses or land;
> I'd rather be led by His nail-pierced hand.

Treasure 4: Incomparable Splendor

The fourth promise Paul brings out in this passage is our hope of heaven. We can have hope in the midst of suffering if we have an eternal focus which is grander than life itself—the confidence that we will one day see the glory and incomparable splendor of the resurrected Christ face to face.

What will heaven be like? There are plenty of Scripture passages which speak of the eternal state in the new heaven and new earth, yet there are still more questions than answers. One thing we can be sure of, however, is this: "The sufferings of this present time are not worth comparing with the glory that is to be revealed to us" (Rom. 8:18).

By focusing on the incomparable splendor and glory to be revealed, Paul is not dismissing the grief and pain brought on by life's troubles. He is redirecting our attention to the hope we have in Christ. Commenting on Romans 8:18, MacArthur says we must remember that "our suffering is earthly, whereas our glory is limitless. Our suffering is in our mortal and corrupted bodies, whereas our glory will be in our perfected and imperishable bodies."[5] The world in which we live is not the final reality. Our ultimate reality is the new heaven and the new earth which awaits the children of God.

Therefore we look forward to the Day of the Lord, when we will see the glory of Christ and the redemption of our bodies. At the resurrection our heavenly Father will "wipe away every tear from [our] eyes, and death shall be no more, neither shall there be mourning, nor crying, nor pain anymore, for the former things have passed away" (Rev. 21:4). But the beauty and splendor of this Day is so much more. "No longer will there be anything accursed" and we "will see his face" (Rev. 22:3–4).

The glory and incomparable splendor to be revealed is beyond the ability of words to describe. The redeemed from every nation will gather around the throne in heaven. The Father will radiate with the "appearance of jasper and carnelian." Around the throne will be a brilliant rainbow with the "appearance of an emerald" (Rev. 4:2–3). The worship of the four living creatures, the twenty-four elders and all creation will never cease. Not only will the Father be on His throne, but the Lamb of God, Jesus Christ, will be at His right hand. "Every creature in heaven and on earth and under the earth and in the sea, and all that is in them" will be singing a new song and saying, "To him who sits on the throne and to the

Lamb be blessing and honor and glory and might forever and ever!" (Rev. 5:13–14). This is the glory to be revealed.

When this is revealed to us, we will be changed forever! "Beloved, we are God's children now, and what we will be has not yet appeared; but we know that when he appears we shall be like him, because we shall see him as he is" (1 John 3:1–2). What trouble is so dark to tarnish this glory? What pain is so difficult to dampen this joy? What trial is so lengthy to compare with the eternal inheritance which is our hope?

God's good and perfect will is not centered on our personal fulfillment and happiness.

It is not difficult to dwell on and be consumed with immediate needs. When bills need to be paid and there is little or no money coming in, what will happen? Will we lose our home? But when we mediate on the splendor of dwelling forever in the house of the Lord, what hardship in this life can compare? These trials are only temporary.

Paul refers to trials as "light momentary afflictions" which are "preparing for us an eternal weight of glory beyond all comparison, as we look not to the things that are seen but to the things that are unseen. For the things that are seen are transient, but the things that are unseen are eternal" (2 Cor. 4:17–18). At first, I did not see the potential impact of unemployment as being a "light affliction." And when the financial struggles stretched out to a second year, it also didn't seem as being only "momentary." This is where we, as the followers of Christ, must keep an eternal perspective. In comparison to all eternity, and the glorious treasure which awaits us when we behold the incomparable splendor of the glory of God in the face of Christ, then even prolonged economic challenges will appear as "light momentary afflictions.

Treasure 5: Ultimate Good

Another source of hope when enduring trials and troubles in life is Romans 8:28: "And we know that for those who love God all things work together for good, for those who are called according to his purpose." This particular promise is not a rallying cry for the prosperity gospel; it does not say (as some would have us think) that God works all things out according to what we consider to be good. It fact, if we equate our temporal, earthly dreams and desires of this life to what God deems to be ultimately good, we miss the heart of God's redemptive plan.

This promise speaks to God's eternal purpose: to bring glory to Himself. Every aspect of God's decrees are aimed at showing forth His intrinsic glory "for from Him and through Him and to Him are all things" (Rom. 11:36). For those of us who love the Lord, what could possibly be more "good" than to glorify God?

The promise of Romans 8:28 points to something far grander than a comfortable and easy life in this world. God's good and perfect will is not centered on our personal fulfillment and happiness. It has nothing to do with getting the "ideal" job or the "perfect" home.

When trouble strikes, we need to keep our perspective, and see trials as part of a plan much bigger than our comfort. I learned the value of perspective when I took an art appreciation course in college. With certain paintings it is easy to get too close and end up focusing on the short individual brush strokes. In order to see the beauty, radiance and glory of the work, you must literally take a step back to capture the fullness of the scene. In a similar way, the trials in our lives are the short individual strokes. We must see them as part of the overall masterpiece which God is creating according to His purposes. God is working all things together to bring about the greatest glory to His name.

The "good" which God is working out from the individual brush strokes of our lives is spiritual and eternal, not material and temporal. We reflect the glory of God by being conformed to the likeness of Jesus Christ. Tough times become the fertile soil in which God grows in us a Christ-like character. Through unemployment God grows us in humility, leads us to repent of our self-reliance and develops in us a deeper trust in His sovereignty. Through the pain of joblessness, God grows us in true joy and leads us to repent of settling for the fleeting happiness of this world. Through a period without work, God grows us in true contentment, leading us to repent of our dissatisfaction, to turn from the treasures of this world and to seek first the kingdom of God (Matt. 6:25–34) and the sufficiency of His grace. To be conformed into the likeness of Christ is truly good. It is a priceless treasure.

Treasure 6: Inseparable Love

Paul caps off the promises in this chapter with this assurance: "For I am convinced that neither death nor life, nor angels nor rulers, nor things present nor things to come, nor powers, nor height nor depth, nor anything else in all creation, will be able to separate us from the love of God in Christ Jesus our Lord" (Rom. 8:38–39). In a chapter which encompasses the high peaks of God's blessings and the valleys of hardship, suffering and trials, the apostle concludes that the pain of life's troubles will never sever the bond of our new life in Christ.

Our Father has chosen and called us by name.
Therefore, what do we have to fear?

What an incredible encouragement to the people of God in tough times! Unemployment, much like other kinds of trials, causes a sense of loss and an uncertainty about the future, which breeds anxiety, stress and worry. In the midst of this, however, we possess the promise that our loving God will never forsake us. Consider what the Lord spoke to the nation of Israel when they were facing difficult times:

> But now thus says the LORD, he who created you, O Jacob, he who formed you, O Israel: Fear not, for I have redeemed you; I have called you by name, you are mine. When you pass through the waters, I will be with you; and through the rivers, they shall not overwhelm you; when you walk through fire you shall not be burned, and the flame shall not consume you. For I am the Lord your God, the Holy One of Israel, your Savior. . . . Fear not, for I am with you; I will bring your offspring from the east, and from the west I will gather you. I will say to the north, "Give up" and to the south, "Do not withhold"; bring my sons from afar and my daughters from the end of the earth, everyone who is called by my name, whom

I created for my glory, whom I formed and made. (Isa. 43:1–3, 5–7).

We are a new creation in Christ. We have been redeemed by the blood of Jesus. Our Father has chosen and called us by name. Therefore, what do we have to fear? What is there to worry about? If the Lord Jesus Christ is our great God and Savior (Titus 2:13), then will He not also be there for us and with us when the currents of life are sweeping over us like a flood? If Jesus Christ suffered and died for the atonement of our sins, will He not also walk with us, side by side, when in the midst of the fiery furnace of affliction and distress? Nothing can separate us from the love of God in Christ Jesus our Lord; we are "more than conquerors through Him who loves us" (8:37).

The Ultimate Treasure: Christ Alone!

The six treasures highlighted are the foundation of our hope, joy and peace. Each treasure has a common element which points to the ultimate treasure of our faith. The treasure of no condemnation is for those who are "in Christ Jesus" (Rom. 8:1). The treasure of eternal and abundant life through the indwelling of the Spirit is only "if Christ is in you" (Rom. 8:10). The adoption as sons and daughters of God, and the eternal inheritance which is the salvation of our souls, is only for those who are "heirs with Christ" (Rom. 8:17). God is working all things to conform us into the image of His Son so that Christ "might be the firstborn among many brothers" (Rom. 8:29). We are rich; nothing can separate us from the love of God, or bring accusation against us, if we are "in Christ Jesus our Lord" (Rom. 8:39).

Each of these treasures of our faith points to the same conclusion: Christ Himself is our treasure.

The shed blood of Jesus Christ has made peace between God and man. Through His sacrificial death, He stood in our place and took the condemnation and judgment that we deserved. Through His death we have been redeemed; our sins have been forgiven and the debt we could not pay was nailed to the cross (Col. 1:20-22; 2:14).

Christ is our all-surpassing treasure, whether times are good or difficult, whether the road is uneventful or filled with hazards, whether we have financial security and a good job or are in need and without work. The gospel keeps before us the treasure of our inheritance: it points us to Christ alone.

When traveling through the dark valleys of life, it is even more vital that we return to the gospel. What we need at such times is an anchor that holds. We need to stand firm on a solid foundation. It forces us to ask ourselves who we are trusting, and where our treasure lies—which leads to the deeper question: *where is my heart?*

If Christ is our treasure, we will count everything else as loss and rubbish (Phil. 3:8). John Piper declares, "God is most glorified in us when we are most satisfied in Him."[6] We are most satisfied in God when Christ is our highest joy and greatest treasure. We can give thanks in all circumstances only if our treasure in life is knowing Christ Jesus our Lord and being united to Him (Phil. 3:10; Rom. 6:5).

Section Four

The Jewel of Ministry

*Blessed be the God and Father of our Lord Jesus Christ, the
Father of mercies and God of all comfort, who comforts us
in all our affliction, so that we may be able to comfort those
who are in any affliction, with the comfort with which we
ourselves are comforted by God. (2 Cor. 1:3–4)*

No one looks forward to trials. We try to avoid them
when we can, and when we can't, we try to get out
from under them as soon as possible. Yet trials are the way
God conforms us into the likeness of His Son. Trials are the
backdrop which allows the treasure of Jesus Christ to shine
before a world without hope (Col. 1:27).

Trials are a means of catching a fresh vision of the greatness, majesty and sovereignty of God. And yet often our
first instinct is to grumble and complain. A. W. Pink stated,
"It is natural to murmur against afflictions and losses. It is
natural to complain when we are deprived of those things
upon which we had set our hearts."[1] For the believer and un-
believer alike, the journey through unemployment is rough

and treacherous road. Many take the fork in the road which leads to wallowing in self-pity, depression and bitterness. But for the follower of Christ, the path we must take is to trust in the sovereignty of God.

God is at work for the good of those who love him. God is at work in the times when things appear to be darkest. When everything seems to unravel, trust in the sovereignty and goodness of God, saying, "Oh, the depth of the riches and wisdom and knowledge of God! How unsearchable are his judgments and how inscrutable his ways!" (Rom. 11:33). Even in the times when God seems silent and our prayers seem hollow, the Lord is at work. The comfort we can take in trials is based upon our future and ultimate salvation and deliverance.

As we walk by faith in unemployment, taking responsibility and doing our part in the job search, trusting in Christ to sustain us and guide us by the power of His Spirit, then we will be consoled and comforted by the mercy and grace of God. At the same time, by the inner working of the Spirit in us to sanctify us by the truth (John 17:17), we will be further equipped to console and comfort others. So no matter where we are along the journey—concerned our job might be next to be downsized or already in the ranks of the unemployed—let us do all things for the glory of God.

Chapter Nine

Love for the Hurting

One day, after months of struggling to make ends meet without a regular income, my wife and I received a card signed, "In Christian love, seventeen families who care." Inside was a check—enough to cover several bills which were due. The depth of love and generosity shown by God's people during this difficult time brought tears to our eyes. Without their support and encouragement, this trial would have been unbearable.

We have seen this caring spirit expressed in many different ways—and each of these blessings seemed to arrive just when we needed it the most. In addition to financial gifts, some have dropped off food or gift cards to local grocery stores.

There were many times when, just as I had reached the point of discouragement, someone would call to see how we were doing or to pray with me. My family also received many uplifting cards and notes, which were constant reminders that we were not alone. Our brothers and sisters in Christ also frequently invited us over for fellowship, or stopped by to visit and pray with us. Most of the time, they were simply checking to see how we were doing.

Unemployment is one of the most challenging periods of life a person will ever face—financially, emotionally and spiritually. The church must be prepared to minister to those who are going through this kind of serious trial. It is not an optional ministry. It is not just a nice thing to do. It is critical. The church must catch a clear, biblical vision of what a ministry of love involves if they want to care for those who are hurting from the trials of life. Such a vision grows out of an understanding of the nature of the church and its role as a sharing and strengthening community.

For at least a generation, we have been steeped in unbiblical teaching that presents a "corporation" image of the church.

The Nature of the Church

For the church to be prepared to build one another up in times of hardship, we must rest upon a strong biblical understanding of the nature of the church. For many of us, this is going to require a radical paradigm shift in our thinking, because for at least a generation, we have been steeped in unbiblical teaching that presents a "corporation" image of the church.

But Mark Dever and Paul Alexander contend that we cannot have any kind of scriptural foundation for ministry unless we deliberately turn from the concept of the church as a Fortune 500 company: "It's not simply another nonprofit organization, nor is it a social club. In fact, a healthy church is unlike any organization that man has ever devised, because man didn't devise it."[1] We need to return to embracing the biblical language of the church as a covenant people, a family and the body of Christ.

The Church as the Covenant People of God

The word most used in the New Testament for church is *ekklesia*—a people gathered together. According to Scripture, the overriding purpose of the people gathered together is to give glory to God; its central work is "magnification—making God's glory appear to the eyes of the world as big as it really is by bringing it into closer view and sharper focus in the form of the local church."[2]

During national calamities and disasters, such as the 9/11 terrorist attacks, Hurricane Katrina and the current economic downturn, the church has an opportunity to fulfill the Lord's command to "let your light shine before others, so that they may see your good works and give glory to your Father who is in heaven" (Matt. 5:16). In order for this magnification of God's glory to occur, the church must be committed to living together as the covenant people of God.

The church is the assembly of those whom God has chosen, called and saved according to His sovereign grace. Therefore, as individual members of the church, we are united together as one community in Christ. But what does it mean to be a covenant people?

This concept of the covenantal community is rooted in the Old Testament. After the Lord had delivered the people of Israel from slavery in Egypt, He proclaimed,

You yourselves have seen what I did to the Egyptians, and how I bore you on eagles' wings and brought you to myself. Now therefore, if you will indeed obey my voice and keep my covenant, you shall be my treasured possession among all peoples, for all the earth is mine; and you shall be to me a kingdom of priests and a holy nation. (Exod. 19:4–6)

In describing the church as a covenant people under Jesus Christ the mediator, Peter uses similar language as is found in Exodus 19:

But you are a chosen race, a royal priesthood, a holy nation, a people for his own possession, that you may proclaim the excellencies of him who called you out of darkness into his marvelous light. Once you were not a people, but now you are God's people; once you had not received mercy, but now you have received mercy. (1 Pet. 2:9–10)

As the covenant people of God, we are called to live and work together. We have one Lord, one faith and one baptism (Eph. 4:4–6). We are called to be holy as our Lord is holy (1 Pet. 1:15–16).

The concept of covenant continues throughout the Scriptures. The prophet Jeremiah is the first to announce the specific promise of the new covenant which is fulfilled in Christ (Jer. 31:31–33; Heb. 9:15). Though there are unique differences between the old Mosaic covenant and the new covenant, the essence of the covenant relationship remains. The language of covenant always speaks of God entering into relationship with those whom He has called; it is the Lord and His people in community living together.

On the basis of the Lord's relationship with His people, He now desires His people to be in relationship with one another. In fact, the essence of our responsibility in the covenant relationship can be summarized in two commandments: "You shall love the Lord your God with all your heart and with all your soul and with all your mind. This is the great and first commandment. And a second is like it: You shall love your neighbor as yourself. On these two commandments depend all the Law and the Prophets" (Matt. 22:37–40).

Therefore, the local church as a covenant community of the people of God must commit to "help each other run the Christian race with integrity, godliness and grace."[3] In an age of individualism and non-commitment, for the church to again fully embrace this will be counter-cultural. If we see the church as something much bigger than ourselves, then we will count others more significant than ourselves and look not only to our own interests but the interests of others (Phil. 2:3–4). This will become more evident in times of trial and hardship. As the church exhibits this covenant relationship in love for one another, including care for the needy and poor without grumbling or questioning, we truly will shine as lights in the midst of a crooked and twisted generation (Phil. 2:15).

The Church as the Family of God

In past generations, when trials such as major economic downturns struck, individuals and families were able to rely upon extended families which lived nearby. Since the end of World War II, the extended family network has broken down; families are now scattered across the country and often cannot provide assistance in tough times. As a result, the jobless person often battles feelings of isolation, loneliness and abandonment in addition to financial struggles. It is in such a culture that the church must provide encouragement, hope and strength to the hurting and afflicted.

For the world to see our good works and glorify God, the church must prove itself to be a functional family in the midst of a sea of dysfunction. The concept of the church as a family points to an intimate relationship. In a healthy family, there is a greater level of trust and commitment shown to the members of the family than is found in other relationships. By means of our new birth, the church is also to be viewed as a family. We are united together as brothers and sisters in Christ. We have been adopted by God and given the right to be called the children of God (Rom. 8:15–17; Gal. 4:5; Eph. 1:5; John 1:12).

The apostle Paul often referred to the members of the church as "brethren." This term stresses the familial relationship which exists among the members. Not only are we brothers and sisters in Christ, but Christ Himself is not ashamed to call us brothers (Heb. 2:10–13). To be a member of the family of God radically transforms our perspective on both the vertical and horizontal planes.

On the vertical plane, the familial relationship we now enjoy with God, through fellowship and union with Christ, gives us the freedom to come before Him and cry, "Abba! Father!" (Rom. 8:15; Gal. 4:6); this denotes a father/son relationship filled with compassion, tenderness and loving-kindness. As our heavenly Father, God promises, "I know the plans I have for you, plans for welfare and not for evil, to give you a future and a hope" (Jer. 29:11).

"Abba! Father!" also gives an explanation for the trials which His people experience. As our heavenly Father, discipline is seen as one way in which God treats us as sons (Heb. 12:7). To be honest, no child enjoys discipline. Discipline can be painful. It is important to understand that discipline is more than just punishment for wrongdoing; it is also training in what is right. Therefore, a loving father will see the value and benefit of discipline and will execute it for the well-being of his children. "For the moment all discipline seems painful rather than pleasant, but later it yields the peaceful fruit of righteousness to those who have been trained by it" (Heb. 12:11). Therefore, we need to see our trials as part of God's ongoing discipline which later will produce the fruit of righteousness in our lives.

The concept of the church as family also has a horizontal dimension. If God is our Father and Christ is our brother, then all who believe in Christ are our brothers and sisters in Christ. If we are all part of the same family, we should love one another. As a matter of fact, love is the one characteristic which Jesus said would mark the church as being His disciples (John 13:34–35). The world should be turning to the church to understand what true love looks like. To our shame, the church can appear just as dysfunctional as many of our earthly families.

The church should be the one place where the world can discover what a truly healthy family looks like.

Families become dysfunctional when pride and selfishness reign. This results in other members of the family being hurt, belittled and even abused. This is true in spiritual families (the local church) as well. As long as the desires of our flesh are allowed to rise up against the desires of the Spirit who indwells us (Gal. 5:16–26), our relationships will become troubled and dysfunctional. Such things as strife, jealousy, fits of anger, rivalries, dissentions, divisions and envy will end up characterizing our relationships (Gal. 5:20–21). The fallout will be hurt, forgotten or lonely people.

This should never be the case. The church should be the one place where the world can discover what a truly healthy family looks like. We ought to go the extra mile in showing love to one another and in ministering to the wounded, lonely and needy in our congregations. This is what healthy families do: they rally around and care for one another when they are in need. Though we are still fallen creatures, we can also shine as lights by the way we forgive and reconcile with one another when we are hurt.

The Church as the Body of Christ

The church is also seen as a body. You do not need to have an advanced degree in anatomy to see how the body is a system of interrelated and interdependent parts. As such, the body perfectly illustrates the necessity and value of each member in the church. The apostle Paul summarizes the significance of the church as a body:

> For the body does not consist of one member but of many. If the foot should say, "Because I am not a hand, I do not belong to the body," that would not make it any less a part of the body. And if the ear should say, "Because I am not an eye, I do not belong to the body," that would not make it any less a part of the body. If the whole body were

an eye, where would be the sense of hearing? If the whole body were an ear, where would be the sense of smell? But as it is, God arranged the members in the body, each one of them as he chose. If all were a single member, where would the body be? As it is, there are many parts, yet one body (1 Cor. 12:12–20).

Many look to this passage to highlight diversity. Yet it must also be noted that the body is a whole; it is a unit. Division is unnatural and harmful. A healthy and properly functioning body exhibits a wholeness and unity. Therefore, in order for the church to shine like stars, it too must exhibit the oneness and diversity of a unified body—caring for one another because "if one member suffers, all suffer together; if one member is honored, all rejoice together. Now you are the body of Christ and individually members of it" (1 Cor. 12:26–27).

These passages from First Corinthians should drive us to strengthen and encourage each individual member in the church. Every member is to be honored and cared for when he or she is sick or suffering, from the elders and senior members to the children, even the nursing infants.

A human body can often function without a particular member working. In fact, many people live well even though they have less than one hundred percent operation of one or more of their limbs or organs. Yet this is not to dismiss the truth that each and every body part is valuable. So if an organ is sick or malfunctioning, or a limb is broken or weak, it affects the whole body because it is not operating at its full potential. That is when we usually call in a physician.

Generations ago the church viewed their pastors as "physicians of the soul." The same way medical doctors work to bring healing to the human body, pastors and elders were seen as the ones responsible to care for the flock which God had entrusted to them (Acts 20:28, 35)—including the sick, wounded and needy members of the church. The church leadership is to have oversight of the individual members, to strive for a church that is healthy, functioning properly and operating at its highest potential—all for the glory of God.

Building Up the Church

The church, as the covenant people of God, serves the one and living God and is bonded together by one Lord and one Spirit (1 Cor. 12:4–6). As the family of God, the church has one Father who is in heaven and is united together as brothers and sisters in Christ. The body of Christ stresses the unity and diversity which exist among the individual members of the church. What unites all three of these metaphors is the emphasis upon interconnected and interdependent relationships among the children of God.

When adversity and hardship strikes, a healthy church will move into action to care for those in need within their congregation. Unlike the social gospel movement, we do not replace sound doctrine with social benevolence. Rather, we express Christ-like compassion, rooted in Christ-centered teaching.

The early church is an excellent example. Notice the progression that exists in Acts 2:42–47. The text begins by stressing how the church "devoted themselves to the apostles' teaching." Flowing from this sound doctrine and Christ-centered instruction was a compassion for one another. This is evident in their fellowship, "the breaking of bread and the prayers." The communal cohesiveness did not end with their public meetings but continued to the point where "all who believed were together and had all things in common." This love and care for one another spilled over into "selling their possessions and belongings and distributing the proceeds to all, as any had need." It is significant that the members of the church voluntarily gave what they could to provide for the needs of others (Acts 4:32–37) with glad and generous hearts. This is the type of giver God delights in and loves (2 Cor. 9:7).

In the New Testament the command to love one another appears sixteen times. This love must be seen not only in "word or talk but in deed and in truth" (1 John 3:18). In other words, love must be expressed in real, authentic and practical ways. This begs the question: How does a ministry aimed at caring for the needs of the unemployed address their varied physical, spiritual and emotional needs? To only provide food is to miss the deep-seated spiritual and emotional hurts and struggles. To exclusively provide biblical counseling and discipleship is to ignore basic physical needs such as food and shelter. Therefore, an effective ministry to the unemployed will include both sharing and strengthening.

A Sharing Community

The idea of God's covenant people being a sharing community is rooted in the Old Testament Law. To love your fellow members of the community included many stipulations for providing for the poor, the widows and the foreigners (Deut. 14:28–29). There is the direct command not to harden your heart toward one of your brothers if he should become poor (Deut. 15:7–8). The people were not to reap the fields to the very edge but to leave some for those in need (Deut. 24:19–22; Leviticus 19:9; 23:22). The Bible also states that God comes to the aid of the poor and destitute, and brings judgment upon those who pervert justice and ignore or take advantage of the poor among them (Ps. 12:5; Prov. 22:22; Jer. 5:28; Amos 2:6–7; Zech. 7:10; etc.).

The early church continued to model this love for those in need, as written in the Old Testament and displayed by Christ in His earthly ministry. In fact, one of the first issues the church addressed was the proper care and provision for the widows within the church (Acts 6:1–6). Paul collected financial resources from the churches throughout Asia Minor to assist in providing for the needs of their brothers and sisters in Christ living in Jerusalem (Rom. 15:25–26).

In order for love to permeate the church, each member must take on a servant's heart.

The testimony of Scripture is to show love for one another by sharing with those in need. A sharing community is not solely about financial giving. A sharing community also sacrificially gives of time and energy in meeting the needs of others. This includes mourning with those who mourn and rejoicing with those who rejoice (Rom. 12:15). Sharing life together also includes bearing the burdens of others (Gal. 6:2) by comforting those who are hurting and praying with those who are in need (James 5:16).

A sharing community consists of individual members who look not only at their own interests but also to the interests of others (Phil. 2:4). This requires true biblical humility—counting others more significant than themselves (Phil. 2:3). Our pride and desires of the flesh war against such a mindset. We constantly are driven to think What's in it for me? How will this benefit me? In order for love to permeate the church, each member must take on a servant's heart. Being a member of a sharing community often means giving with no tangible return and sacrificing without accolades. What could be more counter-cultural for Westerners?

It is also counter-cultural because we are programmed to expect a return on an investment. But a sacrificial investment does not often yield tangible results; the return is spiritual. Giving will not necessarily translate into rising attendance or an increased church budget; in fact, it might even require a greater burden upon the finances of the church. A sharing community, however, is about building up the lives of individuals—which can be spiritually rewarding for the giver.

When the church embraces this kind of vision for caring for the needy, the world will notice, the church will become a beacon of light reflecting the love of Christ, and God will be glorified. "You will be enriched in every way to be generous in every way, which through us will produce thanksgiving to God. For the ministry of this service is not only supplying the needs of the saints, but is also overflowing in many thanksgivings to God" (2 Cor. 9:11–12).

A Strengthening Community

A healthy and biblically functioning church also labors to strengthen and build up one another in love and in the faith (Eph. 4:16). In other words, the goal of this work is spiritual maturity. Trials are a key way in which God works to bring about this maturity (James 1:2–4).

Throughout the book of Acts we see the leadership of the church focused on strengthening and encouraging the members. After the Jerusalem Council the church sent out Judas and Silas for this very reason (Acts 15:32). After Paul had parted ways with Barnabas, "he went through Syria and Cilicia, strengthening the churches" (Acts 15:41). Everywhere a church had been established Paul made it a point to strengthen the believers in their faith (Acts 18:23, Acts 16:40). Even after Paul was stoned in Lystra, he returned into the city for the express purpose of "strengthening the souls of the disciples, encouraging them to continue in the faith, and saying that through many tribulations we must enter the kingdom of God" (Acts 14:22). In this particular passage we see the focus was on learning to suffer well.

To strengthen means to give support. As a boy, I remember my parents planting tomatoes in our backyard. Each plant was in a wire "cage" to keep the plants upright. In a similar way, "strengthening the church" refers to those activities which support and build up individual believers so they are able to stand firm and remain steadfast in the faith, especially during the storms of life.

A picture of this kind of strengthening is seen at a marathon: the runners are handed cups of water to replenish their body fluids and water-soaked sponges to cool off with, as the cheering crowds shout out words of encouragement. Paul used similar scenes from the world of athletics to illustrate deeper spiritual truths. In fact, he even viewed his own life in terms of an athletic competitor. His life was marked with the determined effort to press on toward the goal set before him (Phil. 3:14). In turn he encouraged the churches to also press on toward the prize set before them: "Do you not know that in a race all the runners run, but only one receives the prize? So run that you may obtain it" (1 Cor. 9:24).

Life should never be viewed as a sprint; it is a marathon. We need encouragers to be there for us along the road of life. When the road becomes difficult and the terrain harsh, we need the extra aid and assistance from fellow sojourners. It might be to replenish our drained and weary souls with sound, biblical counsel and wisdom. At other times, when the intensity of life's trials and hardships heat up and leave us weak and exhausted, we need others to come alongside and refresh our spirits by soaking us in prayer and the words of Scripture. Also, regardless of where we are along the road, we need others to spur us on in perseverance. This is what is meant by encouragement!

To be a healthy and biblical community, the church must be dedicated to strengthening one another and building one another up in love and in the faith. We need to be there for those who are hurting and wounded by the emotional, spiritual scars of life's trials. We need to speak words of promise and hope and spur one another along in remaining steadfast in the faith when trials weigh us down. We need to live out the commandment to love one another, not only in word, but also in truth and deed (1 John 3:18–19).

Chapter Ten

Components of a Ministry
to the Unemployed

In the early church the office of deacon was created for the purpose of carrying out a ministry to those in financial need (Acts 6:1–6). But with the advent of social services such as welfare for the poor and unemployment benefits for those who have lost their jobs, some are asking if the church needs to be involved in this area any longer. Is a ministry to people in financial crisis obsolete? John Murray responds with an emphatic no.

> Notwithstanding all provisions for the poor [and, for that matter, the unemployed] in the so-called welfare state, there is ample scope for the exercise of [the ministry of deacons], and the church needs to be alerted to the needs, in some cases appalling, that exist in this area of Christian opportunity and obligation.[1]

The church's ministry to the needy has not been made unnecessary just because of modern social programs. In fact, it is likely that the government's increased role in providing resources to the poor is in part a result of the church's neglect of their calling to be salt and light in the world by caring for those in need.

Aggravating the situation, the American church tends to be programmatic in the way it addresses needs within the church. It is easy to become so consumed with our strategic planning, programs and events that we miss out on seeing how to minister to the whole person.

To avoid this the church—as a covenant people, a body, a family—needs to be marked by deep and sincere love for one another, a love that is seen in deed and truth. But what specific deeds express a genuine and authentic love for one another in the body of Christ? Don McMinn's book, *The 11th Commandment: Experiencing the One Anothers of Scripture*, does a thorough work of explaining how "the mysterious 'how-to' of love is practically explained by the 'one anothers' of Scripture. We demonstrate love by engaging in the One Anothers."[2]

If the church is going to be healthy and biblical, prayer neeeds to be the starting point of any effective ministry of the church.

There are thirty-five "one-another" commands given in the New Testament. Each one gives a different perspective of what it means to love in "deed and truth" (1 John 3:18). Five specific ones are foundational for effective ministry to those who are unemployed and struggling to make ends meet.

Pray for One Another (James 5:16)

It is easy to see prayer as an obvious point and to skip over to more "substantive" forms of assistance. But if the church is going to be healthy and biblical, prayer needs to be the starting point of any effective ministry of the church. Ministry to those in need requires the more specific form of prayer for one another.

But what is prayer? How ought we to pray? Specifically, how is prayer to be a core component in a ministry to the unemployed? The simplest definition of prayer is communication with God; the Lord Jesus gave us a model for prayer. In prayer we are to come before our heavenly Father with reverence because of His awesome holiness (Matt. 6:9), and seek the will of God to be accomplished here on earth as it is in heaven. Prayer is more about asking God to complete His plans and purposes than it is to ask Him to fulfill our plans and purposes. Central to the will of God for our lives is our sanctification (Matt. 6:10; 1 Thess. 4:3). Therefore, one way to pray for one another is to ask God to use the circumstances of life in transforming us into the likeness of Christ.

Scripture also makes it clear that one purpose of prayer is to share with the Lord our needs and requests. This is not to inform God of something He does not know. It is not to pester God to give us what we want. Rather, it is to express our utmost need and dependence upon Him (Matt. 6:11–13). This type of prayer is vital to the life and health of the church; it exalts the sovereignty of God and nurtures humility in His people. But we also need to pray for the specific needs of others.

When others say they will pray for you, do you wonder if they ever do? We all have good intentions, but the busyness of life crowds in, and praying for the needs of others gets neglected or overlooked. I have been guilty of this, and knowing my own shortcomings, I sometimes doubt that others will remember to pray. This is why it is so much more meaningful when someone not only promises to pray *for* you but stops and actually prays *with* you. It is like that sponge of cold water an athlete receives, giving relief in the heat of the race.

During my days of being without a job, my family was blessed to have many who took the extra effort and time to pray *with* us. One night a couple came to visit us, and before they left, the husband asked in a quiet voice, "Can we pray for you before we go?" This was all the more meaningful because this man is quiet and reserved, so offering to pray was outside his comfort zone. Hearing him lift up to the Lord our financial and spiritual needs also had the effect of lifting our spirits. It was such an encouragement.

On another occasion I was the guest preacher at a church. After I finished the senior pastor stood up and said, "I think we should gather around Rich and his family, and pray for them." One by one individuals who we barely knew began to gather around us and place their hands upon our shoulders. One by one they poured out their hearts before the Lord on our behalf, praying that we would experience joy, comfort and peace during the difficult days of my unemployment. My wife and I left that evening in tears—but they were tears of joy! We left with a renewed peace because of the kindness which God showed us through His people; it was the kindness of so many taking the time to pray *with* us.

We should never take prayer lightly; it is powerful and effective in its working (James 5:16). The natural tendency of the flesh is to give up in prayer, after only a short while, if we don't see an answer to our requests and supplications. If we wake up each morning and see no change in our circumstances, it is easy to get discouraged and sigh, "What's the point? Nothing changes." This is where we need to develop perseverance and fervency in prayer. This is also where it is valuable to have someone there to pray with us.

Effective prayer is sincere, passionate and devoted. "The prayer of a righteous person has great power as it is working. Elijah was a man with a nature like ours, and he prayed fervently that it might not rain, and for three years and six months it did not rain on the earth. Then he prayed again, and heaven gave rain, and the earth bore its fruit" (James 5:16–17). Elijah was a man like us, yet what sets him apart from so many us is the intensity and burning zeal in his prayer. He was an ordinary man who served and prayed to an extraordinary God.

The disciples saw this same devotion and sincerity in the life of prayer which Jesus exhibited. They also witnessed the effective and powerful working which stemmed from His prayer life. The disciples made the connection between the power and the fervency of prayer and asked Jesus to teach them to pray (Luke 11:1).

It is unbiblical, however, to see prayer as the equivalent of plugging an appliance into an electrical outlet. The purpose of prayer is not to give us the power to do what we want. This perspective is what often causes frustration in prayer. If we pray and nothing happens as we wanted, then we think something is wrong or doubt the power of prayer.

Notice that James 5:16 states that the powerful working of prayer is linked to being a righteous person. Throughout Jesus' earthly ministry He did only what His Father instructed (John 8:28; 12:49). The testimony of the Gospel accounts is of Jesus spending extended time in prayer and then doing the will of His Father (Mark 1:35–38; Luke 4:42–44). Therefore, the true power of prayer is the Lord transforming our desires and our will to become aligned with His desire and will.

Effective ministry begins with prayer. As a family, we ought to love our brothers and sisters in Christ enough to come alongside them, to pray for and with them. As the body of Christ we ought to show enough concern for other members of the body to bring before the throne of grace petitions of mercy and compassion. As the covenant people of God, we ought to care enough to beseech the "Lord Who Provides" for the basic necessities of those in need—physical, emotional and spiritual. Our prayers will exhibit a dependence upon the sovereign Lord for our needs ("give us this day our daily bread") as well as a hope in the promises of Scripture ("my God will supply every need of yours according to his riches in glory in Christ Jesus.") So, to love one another begins with the commitment to pray for and with one another.

Bear One Another's Burdens (Gal. 6:2)

First Thessalonians 5:14 instructs the church to "admonish the idle, encourage the faint-hearted, help the weak, be patient with them all." We may be reluctant to live out this instruction for fear of being spiritually and emotionally drained. Investing in the lives of the burdened and those weighed down by the hardships of life can be costly.

One reason it is difficult to bear one another's burdens is

that we don't feel equipped to do it. Since we do not know what to say, we often say nothing at all. Or to avoid getting tangled up in the issues, we give pat answers like, "Well, keep your chin up! Things will get better." Regardless of the intent or motive for our response (or lack of response), the result is often the same: our fellow brother or sister in Christ is left to flounder on their own with the burden of life's problems. Instead of helping to make the burden lighter, we add to it.

First Thessalonians 5:14 also instructs us to admonish one another. There are clearly times when this must be done, but even then, we need to admonish with patience. Admonishing is correcting a specific sin by directing the person to the specific Scripture which reveals its sinfulness. It is not telling someone what *we think* of another's situation or what *we think* God wants them to do. It is insensitive to suggest that someone is not working hard enough to get a job, or that they are putting too many limitations on their job search. Making statements like that is assuming we know God's will for another person's life. This is not admonishment; it is being judgmental.

We may also fail to bear one another's burdens because of a lack of empathy. If we cannot relate to another's pain and suffering, we tend to minimize the issue, telling the person to "just get over it" or labeling them as a complainer. Such misguided efforts at admonishment can force the person to withdraw. If we are going to show love for one another, we must try to feel the same sense of loss which the other person is experiencing.

Job's "friends" who came to "console" Job (Job 2:11–13) may be the ultimate examples of insensitivity and ill-perceived admonition toward the suffering person. Most of us have dealt with "friends" like this. The scenario is all too common. You are in the midst of a trial, suffering and perplexed, and someone shows up at your door. They come with the intent to comfort or encourage, but by the end of the conversation, they leave you even more burdened down. They make broad-stroked explanations about why you are struggling and how to deal with the problem. If you try to give a different perspective, they may get irritated and admonish you with sharp and cutting words. They think they speak for God and know God's will for your life. If you don't agree, they accuse you of "putting God in a box" or "not being obedient to God's leading."

To bear one another's burdens is showing compassion and mercy to those in need.

When ministering to those who have suffered loss, we need discernment. There is "a time to break down, and a time to build up; a time to weep, and a time to laugh; a time to embrace, and a time to refrain from embracing; a time to keep silence, and a time to speak" (Eccles. 3:2–8). There will be an appropriate time to correct and rebuke, and a time to encourage and lift up with words of gentleness and kindness. What someone who has just received a pink slip needs the most is a friend to come alongside, put an arm around his shoulder and say, "I will be here for you. Let me travel this journey with you." If, on the other hand, they have been sitting around the house for weeks doing nothing, it is probably time to admonish them with the stern teachings of Scripture on laziness and idleness.

Ministry aimed at caring for the downtrodden and hurting requires the rest of the body of Christ to come alongside and bear their burdens. It is taking the time to sit down and listen to them share what is on their heart. It is crying with them when the pain of life seems too much to bear. It is empathizing with them when they are hurting—putting yourself in their shoes. To bear one another's burdens is showing compassion and mercy to those in need.

Comfort One Another (2 Cor. 1:3–4)

The word for comfort in the Bible is similar to encouragement. We provide comfort by coming alongside those in need and providing aid. We receive ultimate comfort from our heavenly Father, the God of all comfort. In His lovingkindness the Lord consoles the hearts of His children and brings refreshment to their souls.

God comforts His children through the promises contained in His Word. The particular means in which the Lord provides this comfort to His hurting, wounded and lonely sheep is by providing others in the family of God to come alongside and remind them of the treasures and promises of our hope. The truths and promises of Scripture also provide strength to persevere, so that some of our greatest trials in life become the foundation for a stronger faith. In the infinite wisdom of God, as we are comforted in our trials by others coming alongside us and speaking truth and hope into our lives, "we will be able to comfort those who are in any affliction, with the comfort we ourselves are comforted by God" (2 Cor. 1:4).

As I traveled along the path of unemployment, my family was blessed by many faithful believers who came alongside us and reminded us of the deep and rich treasures of promise and hope contained in the Word of God. They also comforted us by sharing how God sustained them through difficult trials in their life. Hearing the stories and accounts of God's persevering grace is great encouragement for fellow sojourners faced with similar hurdles in life.

One couple expressed their love and support in many tangible ways. They took time to provide special treats for our children. They called from time to time to check in on us, pray with us and encourage us with words of truth and hope. The husband had been unemployed at one point, so he understood the emotional and spiritual roller coaster I was on. He was not only able to truly empathize with my situation, but he turned my attention to the truths of Scripture which provide comfort and strength in the heat of the affliction.

This couple's ministry of comfort to us is all the more precious because they were suffering their own trial—long-term physical illness. Yet through it all they continued to exhibit the joy of the Lord.

Regardless of our level of spiritual maturity, when trouble strikes, we need others who have been through the fire to come alongside us. Stephen F. Saint says, "People who suffer want people who have suffered to tell them there is hope. They are justifiably suspicious of people who appear to have lived lives of ease."[3] We who have been comforted by God in our affliction must be ready to comfort others. The bond shared by those who have suffered is a unique connection that provides the comforter with an opportunity to point to our eternal hope and the secure promises of God's Word.

We shouldn't wait until we have "come out on the other

side" before we look for ways to comfort others. Even in the midst of the trial, we can reach out to others in need by coming alongside to encourage them and instill hope. This benefits ourselves as well as others because it takes our minds off our own hardships and puts them in perspective. It also helps us to better connect with one another as fellow pilgrims, walking by faith on the same journey.

You may be surprised at what a simple expression of comfort can do. Your word of encouragement may be just what someone needs to get through the day. Your word of hope may come to a person at the point of despair and become a catalyst to turn mourning into joy. Your reminder of the promises of God may cause someone on the verge of giving up to persevere and press on. We have no idea how the Holy Spirit will use our words to provide comfort.

The blessing of being an instrument of righteousness is that God uses us for His glory in ways we cannot even fathom. This is the beauty of the church living in community: we become a witness of the light of Christ in the midst of a world marked by loneliness, suffering and division. If a church is going to minister to the beaten down and suffering, it must be serious about its calling to love one another by coming alongside and comforting one another with the phenomenal promises of Scripture and our living hope in Christ.

Care for One Another (1 Cor. 12:25)

The church is to exhibit a harmony and unity in which each member has "the same care for one another." This is the testimony of the early church in the book of Acts: "And all who believed were together and had all things in common. And they were selling their possessions and belongings and distributing the proceeds to all, as any had need" (2:44–45). Out of genuine love, the members of the church voluntarily gave what they could so that "there was not a needy person among them" (4:34). This generosity was not legislated; it came from the heart, as an outgrowth of love and concern for one another. They chose to give sacrificially so it could be "distributed to each as any had need" (4:35).

To our shame, the church often joins the rest of society in relying on government agencies to help those in need. We miss out on the joy of voluntarily giving as well as the blessing of receiving. But when the giver gives freely, for the sole purpose of being a blessing, and when the one who receives does so with thanksgiving to God, we bring glory to God as the world sees a tangible expression of love in deed and truth.

> The point is this: whoever sows sparingly will also reap sparingly, and whoever sows bountifully will also reap bountifully. Each one must give as he has decided in his heart, not reluctantly or under compulsion, for God loves a cheerful giver. . . . For the ministry of this service is not only supplying the needs of the saints, but is also overflowing in many thanksgivings to God. By their approval of this service, they will glorify God because of your submission flowing from your confession of the gospel of Christ, and the generosity of your contribution for them and for all others, while they long for you and pray for you, because of the surpassing grace of God upon you. (2 Cor. 9:6–7, 12–14)

During my time of unemployment, I experienced firsthand the sacrificial giving of many who lived out the principles of Acts 4:34–35. We received baskets of food items and fresh vegetables as well as coolers of frozen meat to store in our freezer. One secret giver blessed my family with gift cards to the local grocery store. Every five to six weeks we received a yellow padded envelope in the mail addressed to "The Jensen Family." There was no return address or any other hint as to the identity of the giver. Even as I write this, I get emotional as I consider the depth of this person's generosity. It leads me to "overflow in many thanksgivings to God." This is the power of the church family caring for one another.

The church should be a community with a deep love for one another that is seen in deed and truth.

Isn't this what the church should be—a community with a deep love for one another that is seen in deed and truth? Will we not shine as lights before others, as they see our good works toward one another and give glory to our Father who is in heaven? Is this not what it means to love one another so that the world will be able to know we are the disciples of Christ? The early church faithfully proclaimed the gospel in the midst of a crooked and perverse generation. They also lived the gospel, visibly showing the world the power of God's transforming work in everyone who becomes a new creation in Christ.

A church that is committed to caring for one another will labor to provide for one another. This includes assistance in the basic needs of food and shelter, but it doesn't stop there. Many who are not in a position to give, especially in seasons of deep economic recession, can extend care for one another in other ways, as the Lord enables. Send a card with a note of encouragement. Make a spontaneous phone call to check in and pray with the person. Caring for one another might be as simple as a touch which carries the unspoken words, "I am here for you." It can be an invitation to dinner for fellowship. It can be a work project of a small group or Sunday school class. All of these are examples of the body of Christ in action.

The church is to be a tight-knit, loving community. Without the generosity and care of God's people, I am not sure how we would have made it through this trial. But that is precisely the point: God never intended for us to travel this road alone. Rugged individualism is not a biblical concept. God formed the church in such a way that if one member hurts, the rest hurt as well (Rom. 12:15) and should come alongside and care for them. This is how we show we are disciples of Christ.

Be Kind to One Another (Eph. 4:32)

To walk in the same manner as we have received Christ the Lord means putting off the old self and putting on the new self, created after the likeness of God in true righteousness and holiness (Eph. 4:22, 24). One way the new covenant people of God live this out is by being "kind to one another." Kindness is the act of doing what benefits another person and is in their best interest. Kindness is an expression of grace—showing favor to another, even if they are undeserving. Just as our heavenly Father has shown His kindness in redeeming and forgiving us (Eph. 1:7), we are to show mutual kindness to one another. Is this not what Paul instructs in Philippians 2:1–5?

So if there is any *encouragement* in Christ, any *comfort* from love, any participation in the Spirit, any *affection* and *sympathy*, complete my joy by being of the same mind, having the same love, being in full accord and of one mind. Do nothing from rivalry or conceit, but in humility count others more significant than yourselves. Let each of you look not only to his own interests, but also to the interests of others. Have this mind among yourselves, which is yours in Christ Jesus.

During my journey through unemployment, my wife and I were hurt by some Christians who inexplicably abandoned us. They did not call or visit. They did not take the time to pray *with* us, so I wonder if they ever prayed *for* us. Why do we so often miss the mark of showing kindness toward one another, especially when it is needed the most? There are several possible reasons.

Perhaps the relationship was not as close and intimate as we thought. Those people may have had no idea that we felt abandoned, because they viewed us as acquaintances rather than friends. But in the church our relational ties ought to go even deeper than friendship. We are a family—brothers and sisters in Christ. If we have a misunderstanding of the nature of the church, we will not cultivate the familial relationships with one another which ought to set us apart as a people.

We may also fail to show kindness to those who are hurting because we do not know what to say. We often think the only way to help and show kindness is by solving the problem or fixing the situation. But the greatest expression of kindness we can show may be to simply sit and listen to a person's hurts and struggles.

Lack of a biblical relationship and not knowing what to say or do can be real roadblocks, but the most likely reason we do not show kindness is because we are just too busy. Our agendas, calendars and to-do-lists are full and overflowing. We are pulled in multiple directions. If we are truly honest, we view it as a burden to help others in need. Showing genuine kindness can be inconvenient. It forces us to step out of the routine of our lives.

This mindset is closely related to the sin of pride, which drives us to look out only for ourselves, often ignoring or marginalizing the interests of others. This is not acceptable in the body of Christ. Each member of the church must intentionally look for opportunities to show kindness to one another.

My journey through unemployment has awakened a more sound understanding of what Jesus meant when He said, "A new commandment I give to you, that you love one another.

The antidote to this kind of selfish pride is being tenderhearted (Eph. 4:32). Tenderheartedness is being compassionate or sympathetic toward the one hurting and in need. This involves going out of our way to do a favor for another and shows a gracious and benevolent spirit. The possibilities for each member in the church to show kindness to one another are only limited by one's creativity and love for others.

I am so thankful for the church. I am thankful to God for the many brothers and sisters who surrounded my family with love. At some of our lowest points, the Lord always directed someone to reach out and take us under their wing. There were many who prayed *for* us as well as *with* us. I could name couple after couple who took the time to listen to us. At times even I got frustrated with hearing the same monotonous account, yet no one ever said, "Rich, I am so tired of hearing about how hard this is. Would you build a bridge and get over it already!" With patience and love, brothers and sisters in Christ expressed compassion and kindness, with many going above and beyond in being used of God as His means of provision for us.

I believe the Lord Jesus wanted my family to travel this road to learn the many lessons expressed in this book. By seeing the church in action, it has also caused me to better understand the nature of the church as a body, family and covenant people of God. He has repeatedly shown me that His grace is sufficient and has used His people to be the means of His love. He taught me the treasure of being a part of His household and a part of a biblical, healthy and functional family of God.

My journey through unemployment has awakened a more sound understanding of what Jesus meant when He said, "A new commandment I give to you, that you love one another, just as I have loved you, you also are to love one another. By this all people will know that you are my disciples, if you have love for one another" (John 13:34–35). I don't think the church has done this well. The church often has a reputation of being the most vicious to its own. This needs to change. The church must be called to exhibit manifold expressions of love to one another.

As a body of believers, we need to reinforce our commitment to each other—before, during and after difficult times.

This includes spurring one another on to look for ways to give to others; it means supplying for the spiritual, emotional and physical needs of our fellow brothers and sisters in Christ. The church must be continually reminded of the blessing and privilege it is to be used of the Lord to be a blessing in the lives of others. This is what it means to be a church in action. This is how the church reveals herself as a precious jewel, shining forth the glory of God in a dark world.

Endnotes

Section One

Chapter 1

1. John Piper, *Don't Waste Your Life* (Wheaton, IL: Crossway, 2007), 112.

Section Two

Chapter 3

1. John Stott, as quoted in C. J. Mahaney, *Humility: True Greatness* (Colorado Springs: Multnomah, 2005), 29.
2. Ibid.
3. Arthur Bennett, ed. *The Valley of Vision: A Collection of Puritan Prayers and Devotions* (Carlisle, PA: Banner of Truth, 1975), 321.
4. Ibid., 320.
5. Mahaney, 138.
6. Ibid., 68.
7. Ibid., 89.
8. Ibid.
9. Ben Patterson, *Waiting: Finding Hope When God Seems Silent* (Downers Grove, IL: InterVarsity, 1989), 49.

10. Mahaney, 140.
11. Ibid., 121.

Chapter 4
1. James MacDonald, *Lord, Change My Attitude . . . Before It's Too Late* (Chicago: Moody, 2001), 68.
2. Matthew Henry, *Exposition of the Old and New Testament*, vol. 1 (London: Joseph Ogle Robinson, 1828), 541.
3. Steven Lawson, Seminar on Resolutions of Jonathan Edwards, presented at Quakertown Regional Conference on Reformed Theology, Grace Bible Fellowship Church, Quakertown, PA, Nov. 14, 2009.
4. "Give Me Jesus," African American spiritual, arr. William C. Witherup.

Chapter 5
1. Joseph Scriven, "What a Friend We Have in Jesus" (hymn), 1855.
2. John Piper, *When I Don't Desire God* (Wheaton, IL: Crossway, 2004), 209–10.
3. Ibid., 31.
4. John Piper, *Desiring God* (Sisters, OR: Multnomah, 2003), 99.

Chapter 6
1. Richard Hendrix, quoted in *Leadership Journal*, Summer 1986, 59.
2. John Piper and Justin Taylor, *Stand: A Call for the Endurance of the Saints* (Wheaton, IL: Crossway, 2008), back cover.

Section Three

Chapter 7

1. John MacArthur, *The MacArthur New Testament Commentary: James* (Chicago: Moody, 1998), 24.
2. John MacArthur, *The MacArthur New Testament Commentary: 1 Peter* (Chicago: Moody, 2004), 43.
3. Warren W. Wiersbe, *The Bible Exposition Commentary: New Testament*, vol. 2 (Colorado Springs: Cook Communications, 2001), 340.

Chapter 8

1. H. Beecher Hicks, Jr., *Preaching through a Storm* (Grand Rapids: Zondervan, 1987), 18.
2. John Piper, *Don't Waste Your Life* (Wheaton, IL: Crossway, 2003), 73.
3. John Stott, *The Message of Romans* (Downers Grove: InterVarsity Press, 1994), 216.
4. John MacArthur, *MacArthur New Testament Commentary: Romans 1–8* (Chicago: Moody Press, 1991), 444
5. MacArthur, *Commentary*, 450.
6. http://www.desiringgod.org AboutUs/Our Distinctives/OurMission

Section Four

1. Arthur W. Pink, *The Sovereignty of God* (Grand Rapids: Baker, 1984), 183.

Chapter 9
1. Mark Dever and Paul Alexander, *The Deliberate Church: Building Your Ministry on the Gospel* (Wheaton, IL: Crossway, 2005), 25.
2. Ibid., 26.
3. Ibid., 110.

Chapter 10
1. *Collected Writings of John Murray, 1: The Claims of Truth* (Carlisle, PA: Banner of Truth, 1976), 242.
2. Don J. McMinn, *The 11th Commandment: Experiencing the One Anothers of Scripture* (Irving, TX: 6Acts Press, 2000), 2.
3. John Piper and Justin Taylor, eds., *Suffering and the Sovereignty of God* (Wheaton, IL: Crossway, 2006), 112.

ABOUT THE AUTHOR

Rich Jensen graduated from Luther Rice Seminary with a Masters of Divinity degree. He taught in Christian schools and then served ten years as an associate pastor of a church in southeastern Pennsylvania.

Rich is available for speaking engagements. He can be contacted at:

Rich Jensen
P.O. Box 55
Perkasie, PA 18944
redeemedcreation.blogspot.com

This book was produced by CLC Publications. We hope it has been life-changing and has given you a fresh experience of God through the work of the Holy Spirit. CLC Publications is an outreach of CLC Ministries International, a global literature mission with work in over fifty countries. If you would like to know more about us or are interested in opportunities to serve with a faith mission, we invite you to contact us at:

CLC Ministries International
PO Box 1449
Fort Washington, PA 19034

———————

Phone: 215-542-1242
E-mail: orders@clcpublications.com
Website: www.clcpublications.com

- - - - - - - - - - - - - - - -

DO YOU LOVE GOOD CHRISTIAN BOOKS?
Do you have a heart for worldwide missions?

You can receive a FREE subscription to
CLC's newsletter on global literature missions
Order by e-mail at:

clcworld@clcusa.org
Or fill in the coupon below and mail to:

**PO Box 1449
Fort Washington, PA 19034**

┌───┐

FREE *CLC WORLD* SUBSCRIPTION!

Name: _____

Address:_____

_____

Phone: _____ E-mail:_____

└───┘

READ THE REMARKABLE STORY OF
the founding of
CLC International

Leap of Faith

"Any who doubt that Elijah's God still lives ought to read of the money supplied when needed, the stores and houses provided, and the appearance of personnel in answer to prayer." —Moody Monthly

Is it possible that the printing press, the editor's desk, the Christian bookstore and the mail order department can glow with the fast-moving drama of an "Acts of the Apostles"?

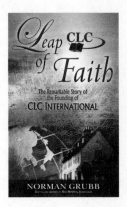

Find the answer as you are carried from two people in an upstairs bookroom to a worldwide chain of Christian bookcenters multiplied by nothing but a "shoestring" of faith and by committed, though unlikely, lives.

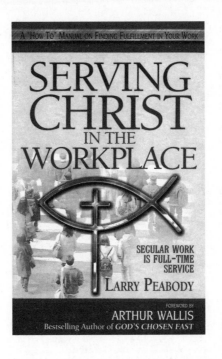

SERVING CHRIST IN THE WORKPLACE

Larry Peabody

Here's a "How to" manual on finding fulfillment in the work God has given you.

"*This book proves that there is no scriptural authority for the belief that serving God in business is any less spiritual than serving God in full-time ministry.*" Arthur Wallis

In the vein of *Practicing the Presence of God* by Brother Lawrence, Peabody focuses on changing **your attitude** toward what you do, not in changing **what** you do.

ISBN 13: 978-0-87508-776-4

WHEN HEAVEN IS SILENT

Ron Dunn

Following the tragic death of his son, Ron Dunn made a shattering discovery—*You can trust God and still get hurt.*

Forced to walk through a painful reality of unanswered questions, he experienced firsthand the processes of grief, guilt and depression.

Gradually gaining new perspectives on suffering as he journeyed toward healing, Dunn shares insights found along the way.

ISBN 13: 978-0-87508-982-9

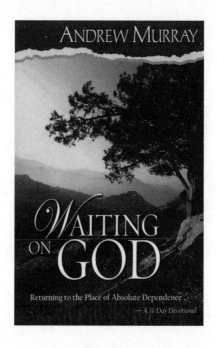

WAITING ON GOD

Andrew Murray

"Has the life of God's people reached the utmost limit of what God is willing to do for them? Surely not!"

With this bold statement, Andrew Murray challenges believers to practice the art of waiting only on God. In thirty-one chapters, arranged as readings for each day of the month, Murray leads us in the school of waiting—of being silent before God in complete trust and dependence.

Invest thirty-one days with Murray in waiting upon God—the results will be more than you could ask for.

ISBN 13: 978-0-87508-854-9

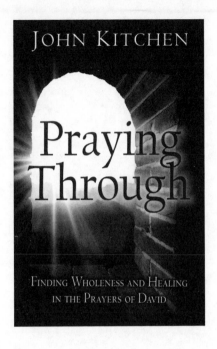

PRAYING THROUGH

John Kitchen

Betrayed? Humiliated? Lonely?
Feeling spiritually dry?

How do you pray when you're spiritually wounded?

King David was betrayed, humiliated, felt lonely and experienced deep hurt and pain on every side. The psalms he wrote
on those occasions are prayers that touch the heart of God. John
Kitchen leads us on a healing journey through those prayers into
a more intimate fellowship with our Father.

ISBN 13: 978-0-87508-978-2